# WHO'S WHO
## *in the*
# BIBLE

### BY DR. STEPHEN MOTYER

*DAVID IS ANOINTED
KING OF ISRAEL*

DK PUBLISHING, INC.

# A DK PUBLISHING BOOK

**Illustrations by Peter Dennis**
**Senior editor** Fran Jones
**Art editor** Jacqui Burton
**Editor** Joanna Buck
**US Editor** Kristin Ward
**DTP designer** Andrew O'Brien
**Production** Kate Oliver
**Managing editor** Anna Kruger
**Managing art editor** Peter Bailey
**Picture research** Christine Rista
**Religious consultant** Dr. Paul Woodbridge,
Dean of Studies, Oak Hill College, London

First American Edition, 1998
2 4 6 8 10 9 7 5 3

Published in the United States by
DK Publishing, Inc.
95 Madison Avenue, New York, New York 10016
Visit us on the World Wide Web at http://www.dk.com

Library of Congress Cataloging-in-Publication Data
Motyer, Stephen Dr.
Who's who in the Bible
   p.   cm
Includes index.
Summary: An introduction, arranged thematically, to four hundred
people from both the Old and New Testaments.
   ISBN 0-7894-2837-7
   1. Bible–Biography–Dictionaries–Juvenile literature.
(1. Bible–Biography.)
BS570.W56   1998
220.9'2–dc21
(B)                                                    97-44747
                                                          CIP
                                                           AC

Color reproduction by Bright Arts (Hong Kong) Ltd.
Printed and bound by Graphicom, Italy

## ABOUT THIS BOOK

*Who's Who in the Bible* introduces hundreds of the main
characters named in the Bible. To retain the storyline of
the Bible, people appear in sequence and they are
also grouped within a themed section, such as
The Twelve Disciples. Bible references for each name
give the book and chapter number where that
person appears, or is referred to, so the reader can
look up the relevant Bible texts. The meaning
of each name is also given, although expert opinion
may vary on the exact interpretation of some names.
All the books in the Bible, together with their
abbreviations, are given below.

### THE BOOKS OF THE OLD TESTAMENT

| | |
|---|---|
| Genesis (*Gen.*) | Ecclesiastes (*Eccles.*) |
| Exodus (*Exod.*) | Song of Solomon (*Song*) |
| Leviticus (*Lev.*) | Isaiah (*Isa.*) |
| Numbers (*Num.*) | Jeremiah (*Jer.*) |
| Deuteronomy (*Deut.*) | Lamentations (*Lam.*) |
| Joshua (*Josh.*) | Ezekiel (*Ezek.*) |
| Judges (*Judg.*) | Daniel (*Dan.*) |
| Ruth (*Ruth*) | Hosea (*Hos.*) |
| 1 Samuel (*1 Sam.*) | Joel (*Joel*) |
| 2 Samuel (*2 Sam.*) | Amos (*Amos*) |
| 1 Kings (*1 Kings*) | Obadiah (*Obad.*) |
| 2 Kings (*2 Kings*) | Jonah (*Jon.*) |
| 1 Chronicles (*1 Chron.*) | Micah (*Mic.*) |
| 2 Chronicles (*2 Chron.*) | Nahum (*Nah.*) |
| Ezra (*Ezra*) | Habakkuk (*Hab.*) |
| Nehemiah (*Neh.*) | Zephaniah (*Zeph.*) |
| Esther (*Esther*) | Haggai (*Haggai*) |
| Job (*Job*) | Zechariah (*Zech.*) |
| Psalms (*Ps.*) | Malachi (*Mal.*) |
| Proverbs (*Prov.*) | |

### THE BOOKS OF THE NEW TESTAMENT

| | |
|---|---|
| Matthew (*Matt.*) | 1 Timothy (*1 Tim.*) |
| Mark (*Mark*) | 2 Timothy (*2 Tim.*) |
| Luke (*Luke*) | Titus (*Titus*) |
| John (*John*) | Philemon (*Philem.*) |
| Acts (*Acts*) | Hebrews (*Heb.*) |
| Romans (*Rom.*) | James (*James*) |
| 1 Corinthians (*1 Cor.*) | 1 Peter (*1 Pet.*) |
| 2 Corinthians (*2 Cor.*) | 2 Peter (*2 Pet.*) |
| Galatians (*Gal.*) | 1 John (*1 John*) |
| Ephesians (*Eph.*) | 2 John (*2 John*) |
| Philippians (*Phil.*) | 3 John (*3 John*) |
| Colossians (*Col.*) | Jude (*Jude*) |
| 1 Thessalonians (*1 Thess.*) | Revelation (*Rev.*) |
| 2 Thessalonians (*2 Thess.*) | |

**Abel** *watches his
sheep while* **Cain**
*works the soil*

# CONTENTS

*Abraham answers God's call and leads his people into Canaan*

## THE OLD TESTAMENT

## THE NEW TESTAMENT

*Jesus talks with the twelve disciples he has chosen to spread his message*

# PEOPLE OF THE OLD TESTAMENT

THE OLD TESTAMENT IS a collection of writing, divided ... ...s, about God's special relationship with the ... people – the Hebrews. The word "testament," ... ...romise" or "covenant," refers to the promises made ...d his people. The writing begins with the creation ...ve and the first broken promise. It traces the ...led history through Abraham, Moses, the prophets, ...gs. It follows their exile and their joyful return to ...land. The Old Testament is the sacred book of the ...nd also forms the first half of the Christian Bible.

*(handwritten, upper left):* When you think you know more or better than the words GOD has given you this is what happens

became corrupted by greed and hatred.

## PATRIARCHS

...rchs are the male leaders or "fathers" of a tribe. The story of ...ham, the first patriarch, shows how God started to deliver the ...orld from sin. He chose Abraham and his descendants to reveal ...the ways of God to the world, but stayed close to them when they ...went astray or fell on hard times. Jacob's sons, shown in this ...family tree, became the patriarchs of the twelve tribes of Israel.

*Abraham and Sarah want to have a large family*

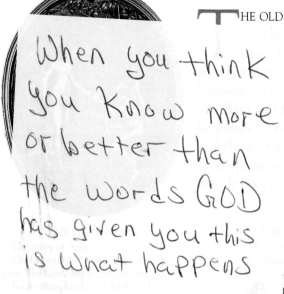

*Isaac and ...ebekah with ...eir twin boys ...u and Jacob*

*Jacob talks with Laban and his daughters, Leah and Rachel*

Hagar        ABRAHA...

Ishmael

*Jacob with sons Reub... and Simeo...*

*(handwritten, center):* So read the Bible for understanding and ~~Knowledge~~ Knowledge (enemy) so you can know who be led (smart) (owl) by

The Twelve Tribes of Israel were descended from Jacob's sons

Bilhah *(& Jacob)*        Zilpah *(& Jacob)*

Reuben · Simeon · Levi · Judah · Zebulun · Issachar · Dinah · Joseph · Benjamin · Dan · Naphtali · Gad · Asher

## MOSES AND THE ISRAELITES

The Israelites became captives in Egypt and were used as slave labor. God heard their cry for help, remembered his promise to Abraham, and sent Moses to lead them out to a new life in a new land – Canaan. He gave them his law to guide them, protected them for forty years on their journey, and brought them to the promised land.

### THE PASSOVER MEAL
Jewish people today share a special meal, called a Seder, at Passover. This meal celebrates the time when God sent a plague to Egypt to kill every firstborn man and animal, but it "passed over" Israelite homes and they survived.

### EGYPTIAN RULE
During biblical times, Egypt was ruled by pharaohs. The pharaoh who oppressed the Israelites was probably Rameses II (c. 1290–1224 BC). Threatened by their growing numbers, Rameses made them slave on his building projects. Finally, he ordered all Israelite baby boys to be drowned.

*RAMESES II AS A BOY*

### THE DIVIDED KINGDOM
Rehoboam failed to hold the kingdom together when his father King Solomon died. The line of David continued in Judah, while Israel was governed by a succession of bad kings. Few of them were able to pass the throne on to their sons.

| KINGS OF JUDAH | REIGN BC | KINGS OF ISRAEL | REIGN BC |
|---|---|---|---|
| Rehoboam | 930–913 | Jeroboam | 930–909 |
| Abijah | 913–910 | Nadab | 909–908 |
| Asa | 910–869 | Baasha | 908–886 |
| *Jehoshaphat | 872–848 | Elah | 886–885 |
| Jehoram | 848–841 | Zimri | 885–885 |
| Ahaziah | 841–841 | Tibni | 885–880 |
| Athaliah (Queen) | 841–835 | *Omri | 885–874 |
| Joash | 835–796 | Ahab | 874–853 |
| Amaziah | 796–767 | Ahaziah | 853–852 |
| Uzziah (Azariah) | 792–740 | Joram | 852–841 |
| *Jotham | 750–735 | Jehu | 841–814 |
| Ahaz | 735–715 | Jehoahaz | 814–798 |
| Hezekiah | 715–686 | Jehoash | 798–782 |
| *Manasseh | 697–642 | *Jeroboam II | 793–753 |
| Amon | 642–640 | Zechariah | 753–753 |
| Josiah | 640–609 | Shallum | 753–752 |
| Jehoahaz | 609–609 | Menahem | 752–742 |
| Jehoiakim | 609–598 | Pekahiah | 742–740 |
| Jehoiachin | 598–597 | *Pekah | 752–732 |
| Zedekiah | 597–586 | Hoshea | 732–722 |
| * Reign of kings overlaps | | | |

## DAVID, KING OF ISRAEL

The Israelites settled in Canaan, where first they were ruled by judges, and later by kings. King David was the second – and also the greatest – of these kings. He was a brilliant military leader, a gifted musician, and proved to be a generous ruler. God promised that David's children would reign over Israel forever. Sadly, after the reign of David's son Solomon, the kingdom split in two – Judah and Israel – although faith in God's promise was never lost.

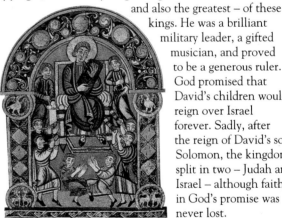

*KING DAVID PLAYING THE LYRE: FROM A BOOK OF PSALMS, C.730*

## THE PROPHETS

Throughout Israel's history God sent prophets to remind the Israelites how they should live. These prophets warned the Israelites of the dangers of disobeying God, but they also spoke of his commitment to them. When the kingdom of Judah was conquered, and God's promise to David seemed to have failed, the prophets spoke of a "son of David" yet to come. Christians believe him to be Jesus Christ.

*PAINTING OF THE PROPHET JEREMIAH, C.1440*

# THE FIRST PEOPLE OF GENESIS

GENESIS – FROM THE Greek word meaning "beginning" – is the first book in the Bible. It describes the creation of the world and the life stories of the first people. It also introduces important biblical themes, such as sin, redemption, wrath, and mercy. It is a story of achievement as well as failure – but finally of hope, as we see God involved in the lives of the people he created.

*IN THE BEGINNING…*
*This illustration from the Lutheran Bible (c.1530) shows the story of creation.*

## GOD'S CREATION

Genesis tells us how God created the world within six days. During this time he created day and night and the sky. Then he made the earth, sea, and plants, followed by creatures of the sea and sky as well as wild beasts. Finally he made man and woman. On the seventh day he rested for his work was done.

## ADAM AND EVE

Meaning: *Man and Life-giving*
Appear: *Gen. 1–4; Rom. 5; 1 Cor. 15; 1 Tim. 2*

In Genesis we learn that God formed Adam – the first man – from the dust of the ground, then breathed life into him. He then placed him in the Garden of Eden with the birds and beasts. It soon became clear that Adam needed more than the company of animals, so God created Eve to be his wife. Adam called her "bone of my bones, and flesh of my flesh!" They both walked naked in the Garden of Eden and felt no shame. Their happiness was ruined, however, when they decided to disobey God. There was one tree – the tree of knowledge of good and evil – whose fruit God forbade them to eat. But they were tempted by a serpent to doubt God's reason for this, and ate the fruit; first Eve, then Adam.

*Adam and Eve pick forbidden fruit in the Garden of Eden*

When they learned about good and evil their innocence was lost and God drove them out of Eden and into the world.

## CAIN AND ABEL

Meaning: *Acquired and A breath*
Appear: *Gen. 4; Heb. 11; 1 John 3*

These were the first two sons of Adam and Eve. Cain, the older, worked on the land while Abel kept flocks of sheep. Jealousy grew between them because God preferred

*Cain kills Abel in a fit of jealous rage*

Abel's offering of his firstborn sheep to Cain's gift of crops. Abel clearly had a better relationship with God. Eventually Cain's anger drove him to murder his brother. God made a mark on Cain's forehead so he would be recognized, and condemned him to wander the earth. In the Bible "to go the way of Cain" means to choose the path of violence and rebellion against God.

## SETH

Meaning: *Appointed*
Appears: *Gen. 4, 5*

The third son of Adam and Eve, Seth was born after Cain killed Abel. Eve gave him this name because she felt that he was a replacement for the son she had lost. She said, "God has 'appointed' for me another child in place of Abel, since Cain killed him".

## ENOCH

Meaning: *Follower*
Appears: *Gen. 5*

Enoch was the seventh generation from Adam, through Seth. Genesis tells us that he lived in close relationship with God, who one day simply took him to heaven. Later legends turned him into a visionary.

*Noah*
*builds a boat*
*from cypress wood*

## NOAH

Meaning: *Comforter*
Appears: *Gen. 5–9*
In an increasingly wicked world, the Bible tells us that Noah was "blameless." When God decided to destroy the world, he wanted to keep Noah and his family safe. He told Noah to build a massive boat, or ark, so they could ride out the forthcoming flood. The ark was also to be a haven for many types of animals. The flood lasted forty days and forty nights and killed all living creatures except those safely inside the ark.

## SHEM

Meaning: *Name, fame*
Appears: *Gen. 5–7, 9–11*
Shem is thought to be the oldest son of Noah, although there is some doubt about this. As a young, married man he entered the ark with his wife and family, and heard the door shut, bolted from the outside by God. Then the rain fell, until the whole earth was covered and the ark floated free. After the flood Shem had a large family, and the nations to the east of Palestine were descended from him.

*Noah's family is safe*
*inside the wooden ark*

*Nimrod*
*oversees the*
*building of*
*the city of*
*Nineveh*

## METHUSELAH

Meaning: *Man of the javelin*
Appears: *Gen. 5*
Methuselah was a son of Enoch and also Noah's grandfather. According to Genesis, the earliest people lived for many years. Methuselah lived the longest of all – for nine hundred and sixty-nine years.

*METHUSELAH*

## LAMECH

Meaning: *unknown*
Appears: *Gen. 4, 5*
Although his children were clever, Lamech was a murderer who taught his wives a song celebrating his refusal to forgive his enemies. Jesus picked up the words of this song when he told Peter that he must forgive people "seventy-seven" times. Lamech's story represents growing civilization, and increasing corruption.

## HAM

Meaning: *unknown*
Appears: *Gen. 6, 7, 9, 10*
Ham was probably Noah's youngest son. After the flood he shamed his father by seeing him naked and drunk, which was forbidden by law. The tribes of Egypt and Canaan were all descended from Ham.

*HAM*

## JAPHETH

Meaning: *Enlarged*
Appears: *Gen. 6, 7, 9, 10*
Japheth was probably Noah's second son. When Ham saw Noah naked, Japheth and Shem shielded Noah by walking backward with a cloak held between them. For this thoughtful action Noah pronounced a blessing on Japheth, picking up the meaning of his name: "May God enlarge the territory of Japheth ..." Japheth went on to become the father of nations to the north and west of Palestine, including the Greeks.

## NIMROD

Meaning: *Mighty hero*
Appears: *Gen. 10; Micah 5*
Nimrod was a fierce warrior and hunter, whose fame lived on in cultures across the ancient world. According to the Bible, Nimrod was the grandson of Ham, Noah's son, who moved east and founded the great kingdom of Babylon. He also built the city of Nineveh, later capital of the Assyrian Empire. Places in that area are still named after him.

## CANAAN

Meaning: *Merchant, trader*
Appears: *Gen. 9, 10; 1 Chron. 1*
The son of Ham, Noah cursed Canaan because he had been humiliated by his father. In the book of Genesis, this curse is connected with the fact that all Israel's enemies were descended from Canaan – the tribes who lived in Palestine before the Hebrews arrived. The area was named after him.

### SEE ALSO

✝ Foreign Kings pp 36–37

# ABRAHAM AND HIS PEOPLE

A BRAHAM WAS THE first biblical leader of the people of Israel. With him we see the beginning of God's plan to deal with the wickedness in the world by revealing himself to people and sharing their lives. God appeared to Abraham and promised to make his name great. Abraham was such an important figure in the history of God's people that he is revered by Jews, Muslims, and Christians alike.

*Isaac* is placed on the altar as a sacrifice

*Abraham* prepares to kill Isaac

## SARAH

Meaning: *Princess*
Appears: *Gen. 11–23; Isa. 51; Heb. 11; 1 Pet. 3*
Abraham's wife Sarah traveled with him from Ur to Canaan and Egypt. She longed for children, but none came. Eventually, following ancient custom, Sarah offered Abraham her maid Hagar to bear children for her. She finally gave birth to her own son Isaac when she was very old. She then banished Ishmael, Hagar's son by Abraham.

## HAGAR

Meaning: *Flight*
Appears: *Gen. 16, 21; Gal. 4*
Hagar was Sarah's Egyptian maid. When Hagar became pregnant with Abraham's child, Sarah was jealous and ill-treated her. Hagar ran away, but God found her in the desert. He made promises about her future son and told her to go back to Sarah.

*Sarah* hears that she is to bear a child

## TERAH

Meaning: *possibly Ibex*
Appears: *Gen. 11; Josh. 24*
Terah was the father of Abraham, Nahor, and Haran. He responded to Abraham's call to leave Ur, and went with his family.

## NAHOR

Meaning: *unknown*
Appears: *Gen. 11, 22, 24*
There were two Nahors in Abraham's family: his grandfather (father of Terah) and his brother. His brother stayed in Ur when Abraham left.

## ABRAHAM

Meaning: *Father of a multitude*
Appears: *Gen. 11–25; and throughout the Bible*

Abraham was born in Ur in Babylon. He was a wealthy nomad, moving around with his huge flocks of cattle and goats. While living in Haran, God spoke to Abraham and told him to take his family to a new home in the land of Canaan. He promised Abraham that all the nations of the earth would be blessed through him and his descendants. This must have seemed unbelievable at the time, because Abraham had no heir. Even his name reminded him constantly of his childlessness. But he obeyed God and eventually, at the age of one hundred, Abraham and Sarah had their son Isaac. They were delighted. One of the tests of Abraham's faith came when God commanded him to kill Isaac as a sacrifice. Abraham was willing to obey – but at the last minute God provided a ram as an offering instead. He praised Abraham for his total trust and dedication.

*An angel tells Hagar she will bear a son called Ishmael*

*Hagar* tells the angel she has run away

*Lot and his family escape from Sodom but must not look back*

*Lot's wife is turned into a pillar of salt*

## ISHMAEL

Meaning: *God hears*

Appears: *Gen. 16, 17, 21, 25, 28*

Ishmael was Abraham's first son, by the slave-girl Hagar. Eventually, pressed by Sarah after the birth of Isaac, Abraham had to send Hagar and Ishmael away. But he loved Ishmael very much, and was comforted by God's promise to make Ishmael's people great.

*Ishmael leaves with his mother*

## LOT

Meaning: *Covering, concealed*

Appears: *Gen. 11–14*

Lot was Abraham's nephew. Seeking adventure, he left Ur with Abraham and quickly became a wealthy nomad like his uncle. They decided to split up and Lot settled in Sodom, the most fertile part of Canaan. Sodom was a wicked place, and Lot had to be rescued from disaster twice, once by Abraham, and once by some angels. Lot and his family fled just before Sodom was destroyed by God. His wife looked back and was turned into a pillar of salt.

## MELCHIZEDEK

Meaning: *King of righteousness*

Appears: *Gen. 14; Ps. 110; Heb. 5– 7*

Melchizedek was the king of Jerusalem and priest of El Elyon. As he returned

from rescuing Lot, Abraham met Melchizedek, whom he recognized as a very special "Priest of God Most High." He gave him gifts, and in turn Melchizedek blessed Abraham.

## ABIMELECH

Meaning: *The king is father*

Appears: *Gen. 20, 21, 26*

Abimelech was the king in southern Canaan when Abraham started living there. Both Abraham and Isaac feared him at first and pretended that their wives were their sisters, in case Abimelech killed them and took their women. But Abimelech proved friendly.

## KETURAH

Meaning: *Incense*

Appears: *Gen. 25; 1 Chron. 1*

After the death of Sarah, Abraham married Keturah, and in his old age had six sons with her. However, he discreetly sent them away so that they would not challenge the inheritance of Isaac, whom he regarded as his chief heir. The sons became the fathers of six Arab tribes living to the east and south of Israel.

ISHMAEL AND HIS MOTHER
*Ishmael and Hagar by Julius Schnorr von Carolsfeld (1794–1874)*

### SEE ALSO

✢ Ben-Ammi p 58
✢ Haran p 59
✢ Milcah p 60

MELCHIZEDEK
*Melchizedek offering bread and wine from the Verdun altar, 1181*

## ABRAHAM'S JOURNEY

Abraham's travels took him a long way. It was 560 miles (900 km) from Ur to Haran, where he stayed until his father died. It was almost as far again to Canaan.

REMAINS OF THE ZIGGURAT OF UR

### The road to Egypt

Abraham moved on to Egypt because of a famine in Canaan. The Pharaoh treated Abraham and Sarah well, but after a short stay he brought his people back to Canaan.

MAP OF ABRAHAM'S JOURNEY

### Abraham's birthplace

Ur was a great center of ancient civilization. Situated in southern Iraq, many spectacular discoveries were made there by archaeologists in the 1920s. The great ziggurat, or temple tower, of Ur was built in about 2100 BC.

# THE PATRIARCHS

T HE PATRIARCHS IS the name given to the first fathers of Israel – Abraham, Isaac, Jacob, and his twelve sons. Abraham was the greatest, the one who first received the promises from God that made the Israelites his chosen people. We now follow the story of the next three generations as told in Genesis.

*Isaac touches Jacob's hairy arms and thinks he is Esau*

## JACOB'S FLIGHT

W hen Rebekah heard that Esau was threatening Jacob's life, she told Jacob to flee to her brother Laban in Haran until Esau's anger had cooled. Jacob stayed for fourteen years before returning for a warm reunion with Esau.

### Desert life
Like his father, Jacob was a nomad who lived in a tent and roamed with his flocks. He prospered in Haran and returned with many goats and camels.

*MODERN-DAY NOMAD'S TENT*

### Jacob's dream
On his journey to Haran, Jacob had a dream in which he saw the door of heaven open and a ladder with angels going up and down. God spoke to Jacob from the top, telling him that he would protect him and make him the father of a great nation.

*STAIRWAY TO HEAVEN*
*This painting by William Blake (1757–1827) shows Jacob's Ladder.*

## ISAAC
Meaning: *Laughter*
Appears: *Gen. 21, 22, 24–28, 35; and throughout the Bible*
When Sarah received the news that she was to have a baby in her old age, she laughed – hence Isaac's name. As a boy he was almost sacrificed by his father Abraham, and learned the lesson that his life depended absolutely on God. Abraham found a beautiful wife for his son, Rebekah, who had twin sons, Jacob and Esau. Esau was the firstborn, but Jacob cheated him out of his inheritance. When Isaac was old and blind, Jacob pretended to be Esau and tricked Isaac into giving him the firstborn's blessing.

## REBEKAH
Meaning: *Enchanting*
Appears: *Gen. 22, 24–28*
Rebekah was Isaac's wife. She was the granddaughter of Abraham's brother Nahor, and traveled from her home near Haran to marry Isaac. She had two sons, Jacob and Esau. She loved Jacob more than Esau, and helped him trick his father into giving him the blessing.

*Rebekah learns she is to become Isaac's wife*

*Eliezer asks God to help him find a wife for Isaac*

## ELIEZER
Meaning: *God is my help*
Appears: *Gen. 15, 24*
Eliezer was Abraham's chief servant and, if Abraham had remained childless, Eliezer would have been his heir. When Isaac was old enough to marry, Abraham sent Eliezer to find a wife for him from among their relatives in Haran. Eliezer prayed for guidance, and God led him straight to Rebekah who agreed to return with him the next day.

## LABAN
Meaning: *White*
Appears: *Gen. 24, 25, 27–31*
Laban was Rebekah's brother. When Jacob went to live with Laban he fell in love with his daughter Rachel. Jacob agreed to work for him for seven years in return for his daughter, but on the wedding night Jacob discovered he had married Laban's other daughter, Leah. Jacob then had to work another seven years to win Rachel.

## JACOB

Meaning: *He grasps the heel*
Appears: *Gen. 25, 27–37, 42, 45–49; and throughout the Bible*

Jacob was the son of Isaac, and the father of the twelve sons from whom the twelve tribes of Israel were descended. He tricked his father Isaac into giving him the firstborn's blessing, by putting animal skins on his arms to make them feel hairy, like his brother's. When he arrived in Haran, fleeing from Esau, he fell in love at first sight with Rachel, who he met at the well outside the town. Jacob eventually had four wives: Rachel, her sister Leah, and their two maids Bilhah and Zilpah. He died in Egypt, where he moved to be with his son Joseph.

**Laban** *rushes to greet Jacob*

**Rachel** *waits at the well while watering her father's sheep*

**Jacob** *sees Rachel and immediately falls in love with her*

*Esau used a bow and arrow to hunt wild animals*

## ESAU

Meaning: *Hairy*
Appears: *Gen. 25–28, 32, 33, 36*

As a newborn baby, Esau was red and hairy all over, hence his name. He was an excellent hunter. One day he came home famished and sold his birthright to his crafty brother Jacob in exchange for a bowl of stew. He was Isaac's favorite son.

## LEAH

Meaning: *Gazelle*
Appears: *Gen. 29, 30*

Leah was the older daughter of Laban, and Jacob's first wife. Her good looks were spoiled by eye trouble, but she bore Jacob six sons and a daughter, including his four oldest sons. There was constant rivalry between Leah and her sister Rachel, Jacob's second wife.

## RACHEL

Meaning: *Ewe*
Appears: *Gen. 29–31, 33, 35, 46*

Rachel was Jacob's only true love, although not his first wife, because he was tricked into marrying Leah. Unlike her sister Leah, Rachel found it difficult to have children. She had to wait while Leah bore Jacob seven children. Eventually she had two sons, Joseph and Benjamin. To Jacob's great sadness, she died giving birth to Benjamin.

## ZILPAH

Meaning: *possibly Short-nosed*
Appears: *Gen. 29, 30, 35, 37, 46*

Zilpah was a maid in Laban's household. When Jacob married Leah, Laban gave Zilpah to Leah as a wedding gift. Later, when Leah thought she could have no more children, she gave Zilpah to Jacob as wife, and Zilpah bore Jacob two of his twelve sons, Gad and Asher.

## BILHAH

Meaning: *Modesty, unconcerned*
Appears: *Gen. 29, 30, 35, 37, 46*

Like Zilpah, Bilhah was a wedding gift to Rachel from her father Laban. When Rachel failed to have children, she gave Bilhah to Jacob to have children for her. When Bilhah had two sons, Dan and Naphtali, Rachel named them and regarded them as her own.

## REUBEN

Meaning: *See, a son*
Appears: *Gen. 29, 30, 35, 37, 42; and throughout the Old Testament*

Leah hoped that Reuben's birth would rekindle Jacob's feelings for her. When older Reuben tried, but failed, to stop his brothers from selling Joseph into slavery.

*REUBEN*

## SIMEON

Meaning: *God hears*
Appears: *Gen. 29, 34, 35, 42, 43, 46, 48, 49*

Jacob's second son by Leah, Simeon killed the people of Shechem in revenge for the rape of his sister Dinah.

## LEVI

Meaning: *Attached, joined*
Appears: *Gen. 29, 34; and throughout the Bible*

Jacob's third son by Leah, Levi's descendants became the priests of Israel.

## JUDAH

Meaning: *Praise*
Appears: *Gen. 29, 37, 38, 43, 44; and throughout the Bible*

The name Jew comes from Judah's name, because his descendants became the biggest tribe of Israel, living in Jerusalem and the area of Palestine that came to be called "Judah." He was Leah's fourth son by Jacob.

### SEE ALSO

✝ The Patriarchs p 4
✝ Bethuel p 58

## ISSACHAR

Meaning: *Man of reward*
Appears: *Gen. 30, 35, 46, 49;*
*and throughout the Old Testament*
After bearing four sons in quick succession, Leah had no more for a while, but gave her maid Zilpah to Jacob. Then, to her surprise, she gave birth to Issachar. The people of the tribe of Issachar lived in southern Galilee, and produced Tola, one of the later judges. Sadly the tribe did not prosper, even though the region was fertile.

## ZEBULUN

Meaning: *Honor or Gift*
Appears: *Gen. 30, 35, 46, 49;*
*and throughout the Old Testament*
Zebulun was Leah's sixth son, and Jacob's tenth. The tribe descended from Zebulun was one of the smallest in Israel, though they produced Elon, one of the later judges. Their land included Nazareth, where Jesus was born.

## DAN

Meaning: *God has vindicated*
Appears: *Gen. 30, 35, 46, 49;*
*and throughout the Old Testament*
Dan was the first son of Bilhah, Rachel's maid. The people of the tribe of Dan lived in the south, near Judah, and caused trouble later when they tried to expand their territory. They were regarded as unfaithful to God.

*Gad is the first son of Zilpah and Jacob*

*Asher is their second son*

**Dan** and **Naphtali** are Bilhah's two sons by Jacob

## GAD

Meaning: *Good fortune*
Appears: *Gen. 30, 35, 46, 49;*
*and throughout the Old Testament*
Gad was the first son of Zilpah and Jacob. The tribe of Gad did not enter the promised land with the other tribes, but stayed on the more fertile eastern side of the River Jordan.

## ASHER

Meaning: *Happy*
Appears: *Gen. 30, 35, 46; and*
*throughout the Old Testament*
Asher was Zilpah's second son, and his name describes her reaction to his birth. The tribe of Asher settled in the fertile region between Galilee and the coast, but became rather isolated.

## NAPHTALI

Meaning: *Wrestler*
Appears: *Gen. 30, 35, 46, 49;*
*Matt. 4; and throughout*
*the Old Testament*
Naphtali was the second son of Bilhah and Jacob. Rachel named him, saying, "I have wrestled with my sister, and won!" The people of Naphtali settled in northern Galilee. Capernaum, where Jesus lived, was in their territory.

## BENJAMIN

Meaning: *Son of the right hand*
Appears: *Gen. 35, 42–46, 49;*
*and throughout the Bible*
Jacob's favorite wife Rachel finally bore him two sons. Joseph was their first son and Benjamin their second. Sadly Rachel died while giving birth to Benjamin. Several years later Benjamin went to Egypt with his brothers to buy food during the famine. Unknown to them, Joseph had become a chief minister there. Joseph decided to test his brothers to see if they would treat Benjamin in the same poor way they had treated him. He accused Benjamin of stealing a silver cup, which would result in his enslavement. When Judah offered to take Benjamin's place, Joseph tearfully revealed his true identity.

## DINAH

Meaning: *One who judges*
Appears: *Gen. 30, 34, 46*
Dinah, Jacob's only daughter, was born to Leah. On a visit to some Canaanite women, she was

*DINAH*

raped by Shechem, son of the local ruler. Shechem then agreed to marry her, but Dinah's brothers Simeon and Levi tricked Shechem and attacked the town, killing all the men. Jacob was very upset by this.

*JACOB REFUSING TO RELEASE BENJAMIN*
*This painting by Roger Adolphe (1800–80) reveals Jacob's reluctance to let Benjamin go to Egypt with his brothers.*

_Joseph_ leaves
his cloak
behind as he
runs away

_Potiphar's wife uses
Joseph's cloak as
evidence that
he seduced her_

## JOSEPH

Meaning: _God adds_
Appears: _Gen. 30,
33, 37–50; Acts 7;
and throughout the
Old Testament_

Joseph was Jacob's favorite, the first son of his much-loved Rachel. When Jacob made Joseph his heir, although he was almost the youngest, he became arrogant and bossy. His brothers hated him, and when an opportunity arose they sold him into slavery, pretending to Jacob that he had been killed. Joseph was not only enslaved in Egypt, he was also unjustly accused of trying to rape his master's wife. God rescued him by enabling him to interpret dreams and Joseph went straight from prison to becoming one of the chief ministers of Egypt.

_Pharaoh
presents Joseph
with fine gifts_

## ASENATH

Meaning: _Servant of the
goddess Neith_
Appears: _Gen. 41, 46_

When Joseph rose to fame in Egypt, Pharaoh gave him Asenath to be his wife. She was the daughter of Potiphera, and became the mother of Ephraim and Manasseh. Later, Jewish experts were puzzled that the mother of two of the patriarchs had been a worshipper of Egyptian gods.

## MANASSEH

Meaning: _One who
causes to forget_
Appears: _Gen. 41, 46, 48; and
throughout the Old Testament_

Joseph and Asenath's first son allowed Joseph to feel that he had been "caused to forget" the troubles of his lost family. Manasseh's descendants included Israel's fifth judge, Gideon.

_Asenath
is given to
Joseph as
his wife_

_Manasseh
and **Ephraim**
are their
two sons_

## EPHRAIM

Meaning: _Fruitful_
Appears: _Gen. 41, 46, 48; and
throughout the Old Testament_

Ephraim was Joseph and Asenath's second son. In his old age Jacob blessed Joseph's sons, and prophesied that Ephraim, though younger, would be greater. This came true when his descendants became the second most powerful tribe after that of Judah.

## POTIPHERA

Meaning: _He whom Ra has given_
Appears: _Gen. 41, 46_

The father of Asenath, who became Joseph's father-in-law, Potiphera was a priest in the Egyptian city of Heliopolis, northeast of Cairo. His name tells us that he served the Egyptian Sun-god Ra. Although the priestly families of Ra were wealthy and powerful, neither Potiphera nor Asenath herself had any choice about her husband. Pharaoh had all the power.

## POTIPHAR

Meaning: _He whom Ra has given_
Appears: _Gen. 37, 39_

Potiphar was the captain of Pharaoh's guard who bought Joseph as a slave. He quickly saw Joseph's qualities and entrusted him to his household. But when Potiphar's wife falsely accused Joseph of trying to seduce her, Potiphar had him thrown into prison.

POTIPHAR

### SEE ALSO

✝ Gideon p 19
✝ Tola p 19
✝ Shechem p 61

## JOSEPH'S COAT OF MANY COLORS

Jacob showed that Joseph was his favorite son by giving him a coat of many colors. It must have been a fine garment, possibly with extra-long sleeves. This indicated that Joseph was not expected to do any dirty work, and marked him out as Jacob's heir.

Joseph dreamed that one day his family would bow down before him, but his brothers hated this idea. It came true when they bowed to an unrecognized Egyptian minister – Joseph.

_**Joseph** tries on his
coat of many colors_

# MOSES AND THE ISRAELITES

MOSES WAS THE greatest prophet in Israel's history. Although Jacob and his family chose to go to Egypt, they soon became slaves there. God called on Moses to rescue the Israelites from Egypt, then revealed his laws to him on Mount Sinai. Here we meet Moses's family and the close helpers who traveled with him.

*Pharaoh's daughter needs a nurse to feed the baby boy*

*Miriam says her mother, Jochebed, can nurse Moses*

**Jochebed**

**Moses** *receives the ten commandments of the law*

## MOSES

Meaning: *Child (in Egyptian) and Drawn out (in Hebrew)*
Appears: *Exodus; and 800 verses throughout the Bible*

Though the Israelites were useful slaves, the Egyptians felt threatened because there were so many of them, and ordered all baby boys to be killed. After three months of hiding her baby at home, Moses's mother placed him in a basket and hid him among the reeds that grew beside the Nile River. Amazingly, Pharaoh's daughter found Moses and decided to adopt him. She even, unknowingly, hired Moses's mother to look after him. Moses grew up as an Egyptian prince. As a young man he became concerned about his people, but had to flee Egypt and work for forty years in the desert. God spoke to Moses from within a burning bush and told him to go back and lead the Israelites out of captivity. Sadly, he never reached the promised land, but died just before the Israelites finally crossed the Jordan River and entered into Canaan.

## MIRIAM

Meaning: *Bitterness*
Appears: *Exodus 2, 15; Num. 12, 20; Micah 6*

Miriam was Moses's older sister. When her mother hid Moses in the river, Miriam kept watch. As soon as Pharaoh's daughter found the baby and fell in love with him, quick-witted Miriam offered to find a nurse – Moses's own mother. Miriam helped Moses lead Israel out of Egypt, using her gift as a prophetess. Exodus 15 records her prophecy about crossing the Red Sea.

## AARON

Meaning: *unknown*
Appears: *Exodus; and more than 300 verses in the Bible*

Aaron was Moses's older brother. Because he was a good speaker, God sent him with Moses to ask Pharaoh to let the Israelites go. God also gave him miracles to perform before Pharaoh. Later he became the first chief priest, in charge of all the worship of Israel.

## ZIPPORAH

Meaning: *Swallow*
Appears: *Exodus 2, 4, 18*

Zipporah was Moses's wife. When Moses fled from Egypt, he stopped by a well and helped seven sisters draw water for their sheep. The girls took him home, and Moses arranged to marry one of them. Zipporah and Moses had two sons. When Moses started on his dangerous mission back to Egypt, Zipporah and the boys set off with him, but later he sent them home to stay with her father, Jethro.

**Aaron** *turns his staff into a serpent to impress Pharaoh*

## JETHRO

Meaning: *Preeminence, excellence*
Appears: *Exodus 2–4, 18*
Jethro was Moses's father-in-law, the father of Zipporah and her six sisters. He was a priest in Midian, a desert area east of Egypt, and owned large flocks of sheep that Moses tended. When Moses and the Israelites left Egypt, Jethro brought Zipporah and her boys to meet Moses at Mount Sinai, and offered him advice about how to lead Israel.

## MOSES AND THE EXODUS

The Exodus was the greatest event in the history of the Israelites. After suffering a series of plagues from God, Pharaoh eventually let Moses lead Israel away. Then he changed his mind and pursued them. God caused the waters of the Red Sea to part before Moses, and his people went through. But the waters closed over the pursuing Egyptian army, and drowned them. A burning cloud, which shone at night, led the Israelites to the Red Sea and through the desert.

*MOSES PARTING THE RED SEA*
*This image by Siegfried Detler (1786–1864)*
*shows the retreating waters of the Red Sea.*

*JETHRO*

## HUR

Meaning: *possibly Boy*
Appears: *Exodus 17, 24, 31*
Hur was an elder of the tribe of Judah and a close associate of Moses and Aaron. After leaving Egypt, the Israelites were attacked by the Amalekites. Hur and Aaron held up Moses's hands in prayer and victory was won. Hur was Bezalel's grandfather.

## BEZALEL

Meaning: *Under the shadow of God*
Appears: *Exodus 31, 35–38; 2 Chron. 1*
Bezalel was skilled at craftwork – he could work metals, carve wood, and weave cloth. He was asked to make all the decorations for the tabernacle, a portable shrine that was used by the Israelites during their wilderness wanderings.

## KORAH

Meaning: *Bald*
Appears: *Num. 16, 26, 27*
Korah, with his friends Dathan and Abiram, led a rebellion against Moses and Aaron during the wilderness years. God acted, and the earth opened up and swallowed Korah, his friends, and their families.

## ELEAZAR

Meaning: *God has helped*
Appears: *Exodus 6, 28; Lev. 10; Num. 3, 16, 19, 20, 26, 27, 31; Josh. 19*
Eleazar was the son of Aaron. When his father died, Eleazar became the chief priest, and also Moses's chief assistant.

## PHINEHAS

Meaning: *Black-skinned*
Appears: *Exodus 6; Num. 25, 31; Josh. 22, 24; Judg. 20*
Phinehas was a son of Eleazar. When some Israelites started to worship idols instead of God, Phinehas killed them. After his father's death, he became the chief priest at Bethel.

## CALEB

Meaning: *Dog*
Appears: *Num. 13, 14, 26, 32; Josh. 14, 15*
Caleb, from Judah's tribe, was part of the group that explored the promised land before the Israelites entered it. Although told that the land could not be conquered, Caleb and Joshua had faith that God would help. Only Caleb and Joshua were eventually allowed to enter the land.

*Joshua* takes
the Israelites
into battle

## JOSHUA

Meaning: *The Lord saves*
Appears: *Exodus 17, 24, 32, 33; Num. 14, 26; Josh; Judg. 2*
Joshua was Moses's assistant, and was entrusted with difficult tasks, such as leading the army against the Amalekites. Before Moses died, God told him to appoint Joshua as his successor. Joshua took responsibility for leading the people into Canaan and establishing them in new homes there.

## ACHAN

Meaning: *unknown*
Appears: *Josh. 7, 22; 1 Chron. 2*
People later remembered Achan as Achar, which means "man of trouble." He was given this name because he stole some of the loot from Jericho, even though God had ordered everything to be destroyed. Because of his disobedience, Israel was defeated in battle. When Achan's theft was found out, he and his entire family were buried under a great pile of stones.

*ACHAN*
*Achan's death: from an engraving*
*by Gustave Doré (1832–83)*

### SEE ALSO

✝ The Amalekites p 17
✝ Gershom p 59
✝ Jochebed p 60

# FRIENDS AND FOES

THROUGHOUT THEIR long history, the Israelites were surrounded by other nations and tribes. Some of these were friendly and lived in peace alongside them. But more often their neighbors were hostile, and some even tried to crush the Israelites out of existence. Here are some of these neighbors – both friends and foes – stretching from the time of the wanderings in the wilderness through to the time of the kings.

*Balak tells his men to find the prophet Balaam*

*Guards stand by to protect the king*

*KNG SIHON*

## SIHON

Meaning: *unknown*
Appears: *Num. 21, 32; Deut. 1–4*
Sihon was a king of the Amorites – a people who lived just to the east of the Dead Sea. The Israelites wanted to pass peacefully through Sihon's territory on their way to the promised land, but the king refused to let them and marched out against them with his army. Sihon was defeated and the Israelites took over his territory. Later, the tribes of Gad, Reuben, and Manasseh lived there.

## BALAK

Meaning: *The devastator*
Appears: *Num. 22–24; Josh. 24; Micah 6*
After the Israelites had defeated Sihon, Balak the king of Moab threatened them. Rather than fight, he tried to persuade Balaam, a local prophet, to put a curse on Israel. Balaam refused. But then, to Balak's horror, he blessed Israel instead. During the reign of David, all Balak's territory belonged to Israel.

## BALAAM

Meaning: *Lord of the people*
Appears: *Num. 22–24; Deut. 23; Josh. 24*
Balak, king of the Moabites, summoned Balaam to come and curse Israel. Balaam consulted God, who told him to refuse, but he was tempted by the offer of silver and gold, and went. On his journey, an angel barred his way. Balaam's donkey could see the angel, but he could not, and he beat the animal. When the donkey spoke, Balaam saw the angel. In the end, Balaam blessed the Israelites instead of cursing them.

*Balaam cannot see the angel standing in the road*

## RAHAB

Meaning: *Broad, spacious*
Appears: *Josh. 2, 6; Matt. 1; Heb. 11; James 2*
Rahab was a prostitute in Jericho. When the Israelites were about to cross the

*Rahab helps the spies escape*

Jordan River, Joshua sent two spies into Jericho. When the king heard the men were in his city, he asked Rahab to bring them to him. Instead she helped them escape from her window in the city wall. Later, when the wall of Jericho fell down, Rahab's house was the only part left standing, and she was praised for helping.

*Jael drives a tent peg through Sisera's head*

## SISERA

Meaning: *unknown*

Appears: *Judg. 4, 5; 1 Sam. 12; Ps. 83*

Sisera was one of the kings of Canaan who fought against Israel. He had nine hundred iron chariots in his army, but it rained on the day of the battle and they got stuck in the mud. Sisera was murdered by Jael.

## JABIN

Meaning: *One who is perceptive*

Appears: *Judg. 4*

Jabin was king of Hazor in Canaan. When the Israelites failed to obey God, Jabin gained control over them. When the Israelites prayed to God, Jabin's army was defeated.

*Agag, the Amalekite king, is killed by Samuel*

## JAEL

Meaning: *Wild goat*

Appears: *Judg. 4*

After defeat by the Israelites, Sisera took refuge in the tent of Heber the Kenite. Heber's wife Jael lulled Sisera to sleep, then hammered a peg through his head. The Kenites always lived at peace with Israel, because they were descended from Moses's father-in-law Jethro.

## ACHISH

Meaning: *The king gives*

Appears: *1 Sam. 21, 27–29*

When David was fleeing from Saul, he took refuge with Achish, the Philistine king of Gath. Achish came to trust David and made him his bodyguard. He even gave David and his men a city to live in. But David avoided fighting with Achish against the Israelites, and even plundered Philistine towns.

## AGAG

Meaning: *unknown*

Appears: *1 Sam. 15*

Because the Amalekites fought against Israel after they left Egypt, God told King Saul to destroy them all. Samuel grew angry with Saul, because he spared King Agag's life. Samuel killed Agag, saying "As your sword has made women childless, so will your mother be childless among women."

## THE AMALEKITES

Moses warned the Israelites that they would have to control the Amalekites after entering the promised land. King Saul tried to subdue them, but failed to destroy them completely. David continued the fight against them.

### A warrior tribe

The Amalekites were a fierce and warlike people. They fought against the Israelites just after they had crossed the Red Sea. During the time of the judges, the Amalekites tried twice to conquer Israel.

*AMALEKITE This 12th-century mosaic shows a warrior in action*

### The promised land

Canaan is the ancient name for the land east of the Mediterranean Sea. This fertile area lay on many important trade routes, and over the years people fought for control of this desirable place.

*THE FERTILE LANDS OF MODERN-DAY CANAAN*

*Namaan washes in the Jordan River*

## HIRAM

Meaning: *My brother is exalted*

Appears: *2 Sam. 5; 1 Kings 5, 9*

Hiram was king of Tyre during the reigns of David and Solomon. He helped them both by supplying materials for David to build his palace, and later for Solomon to build the temple in Jerusalem. To express his thanks, Solomon transferred twenty villages into Hiram's kingdom.

## NAAMAN

Meaning: *Pleasant*

Appears: *2 Kings 5; Luke 4*

Naaman was the commander of the Syrian army, even though he had leprosy. An Israelite slave-girl, captured earlier by a Syrian raiding party, told Naaman's wife about the healing powers of the prophet Elisha in Israel, and so Naaman went to Israel to find Elisha. Elisha told him to wash seven times in the Jordan River, and he was completely cured. Naaman was so delighted that he decided to worship the God of Israel, rather than the god of the Syrians.

### SEE ALSO

✝ Samuel p 21

✝ Elisha p 22

✝ David p 27

✝ Heber p 59

# TIME OF THE JUDGES

AFTER THE ISRAELITES had entered the promised land, they were governed by judges – who were usually warriors and powerful leaders. When the Israelites were unfaithful to God, he let them fall under the power of an enemy. The book of Judges describes how the Israelites repented and how God sent judges to their rescue.

SHAMGAR

*KING EGLON*
This 14th-century image shows the death of King Eglon

*Ehud takes a sword from under his cloak*

## SHAMGAR
Meaning: *Given by Shimike*
Appears: *Judg. 3, 5*
Shamgar ruled after Ehud, when Israel had fallen under the power both of Jabin, a Canaanite king, and also of the Philistines. Life was so bad for the Israelites that they had stopped traveling on the main roads to avoid robbers. Shamgar killed six hundred Philistines using an ox-goad (a long, metal-tipped stick), but could do nothing to stop Jabin.

## DEBORAH
Meaning: *Bee*
Appears: *Judg. 4, 5*
Jabin ruled over Israel for twenty years. When the Israelites could bear it no longer, they prayed to God who spoke to the judge and prophetess Deborah. She ordered Barak to raise a surprise army against Jabin from the northern tribes of Naphtali and Zebulun. Barak was unwilling to do this unless Deborah went with him. After the battle, Deborah sang her famous victory song.

## BARAK
Meaning: *Lightning*
Appears: *Judg. 4, 5; 1 Sam. 12; Heb. 11*
Barak was a young warrior from the tribe of Naphtali. Prompted by Deborah, he raised an army of ten thousand men from his own tribe and from neighboring Zebulun, and defeated the Canaanite army led by King Sisera. Although Sisera had nine hundred iron chariots, God caused heavy rains to fall and the chariots got stuck in the mud. Even Sisera was forced to flee on foot. After the victory, Barak and Deborah ruled Israel together for forty peaceful years.

*Deborah tells Barak to organize an army to defeat Jabin and the Canaanites*

## OTHNIEL
Meaning: *Powerful one*
Appears: *Josh. 15; Judg. 1, 3*
Othniel was the first of the judges. Soon after arriving in Canaan, the Israelites starting worshipping Canaanite gods and so God sent a Syrian king called Cushan-Rishathaim to rule over them for eight years. As soon as they repented and cried to God for deliverance, he inspired Othniel to raise an army and defeat the Syrians. Othniel then ruled Israel for forty years until he died.

## EHUD
Meaning: *Strong*
Appears: *Judg. 3, 4*
Ehud was a Benjaminite judge when King Eglon of Moab was sent by God to invade the land. After years of unhappy rule, Ehud went to pay his taxes to King Eglon with a sword hidden under his cloak. Ehud was left-handed, so Eglon suspected nothing as Ehud reached for his sword and killed the king. Ehud defeated the remaining Moabites, and ruled peacefully for a long time.

## GIDEON

Meaning: *One who strikes blows*
Appears: *Judg. 6–8; Heb. 11*
Gideon was the judge who delivered Israel from the Midianites. He did not realize he was to be a leader until God sent an angel to tell him. Prompted by the angel, Gideon bravely destroyed his father's altar to Baal and cut down the statue of the goddess Asherah next to it. Then he raised an army. God told him to send away all but three hundred men so that he would

*Gideon* destroys the statue of Asherah, a fertility goddess

## WORSHIPPING BAAL

When the Israelites arrived in Canaan they found the people worshipped many different gods. These were known together as "the Baals" (Baal meaning "master" or "lord"). Generally, people prayed to them when they wanted rain to secure good harvests. Sometimes the worship could be cruel, involving adult and child sacrifices. So strong was the local belief in Baal, that some Israelites joined in. This was a problem during the time of the judges, and throughout Israel's entire history.

BAAL WITH A THUNDERBOLT
*A stone relief from Ugarit, Syria*

have to rely on God's power. The remaining men quietly surrounded the Midianite army at night, then suddenly they blew their trumpets and waved torches. Confused, the Midianites fought each other in the dark and fled.

## ABIMELECH

Meaning: *My father is king*
Appears: *Judg. 9*
Disaster struck the family of Gideon after his death. His seventy sons were all murdered in one day by Abimelech, their half-brother. But Abimelech's youngest brother, Jotham, managed to escape and prophesied that God's judgment would fall on Abimelech. After three years Abimelech's misrule came to an abrupt end when a woman dropped a millstone on his head while he was trying to burn down a tower full of people. Jotham's prophecy had come true.

## TOLA

Meaning: *Wearer of purple*
Appears: *Judg. 10*
Tola was a judge who brought some stability to Israel after the time of Abimelech. He came from the tribe of Issachar, and ruled Israel in Shamir

*Jephthah* is horrified when he sees his daughter

(possibly Samaria, where the kings of Israel later reigned). He was followed by another minor judge, Jair, who came from Gilead on the east side of the River Jordan. Jair ruled through his thirty sons. They traveled by donkey, a sign of wealth and power.

## JEPHTHAH

Meaning: *God will set free*
Appears: *Judg. 11, 12; 1 Sam. 12; Heb. 11*
Jephthah led Israel against the Ammonites, who had taken over his home area of Gilead. He vowed that if God made him victor, he would sacrifice the first thing to greet him on his return. Jephthah was victorious – but to his horror his only daughter came out to meet him. He kept his vow and sacrificed her, after she had spent two months mourning her fate with friends. Later, Jephthah caused a civil war in Israel.

## IBZAN

Meaning: *Swift*
Appears: *Judg. 12*
Ibzan was the first of three minor judges who ruled Israel after Jephthah. A wealthy man with thirty sons and thirty daughters, Ibzan ruled for seven years from Galilee. After his death, he was followed by Elon and Abdon.

JEPHTHAH

### SEE ALSO

+ Issachar p 12
+ Sisera p 17
+ Jair p 59

*Delilah reveals that Samson's strength lies in his hair*

*Samson's hair was cut while he slept*

## MICAH

Meaning: *Who is the Lord?*
Appears: *Judg. 17, 18*
The story of Micah shows how confused and lawless Israel was becoming without a king. Micah stole some silver coins from his mother, then returned them. She was so pleased she made them into a silver idol. Micah built a shrine for the idol and appointed his own priest. Then the priest stole the idol and ran away with some bandits from the tribe of Dan, who were looking for a city to capture. The priest lied and said that God approved of their action.

## SAMSON

Meaning: *Man of the Sun*
Appears: *Judg. 13–16; Heb. 11*
Samson is the most famous judge, best known for the massive strength that enabled him, for instance, to uproot the city gates at Gaza and carry them to the top of a hill. When the Israelites fell under the power of the Philistines, Samson could easily have saved them. Instead he misused his strength and ended his days weak, blinded, and in chains in a Philistine dungeon. He prayed for one last chance, which he used to push down the supporting pillars of a temple, killing his enemies and himself.

## MANOAH

Meaning: *Rest*
Appears: *Judg. 13, 14*
Manoah was Samson's father. Although his wife was childless, one day an angel appeared and told her that she would have a special son who would save Israel from the Philistines. Manoah wanted the angel to appear to him too, and eventually this happened.

## DELILAH

Meaning: *Flirt*
Appears: *Judg. 16*
Samson fell in love with Delilah, who was paid by the Philistine leaders to find out the secret of his strength. He eventually told her: his hair had never been cut as a symbol of his special relationship with God. She lulled him to sleep, and cut off his hair. When the Philistines bound him, he could not shake them off. His strength was gone.

*Ruth washes and perfumes herself for Boaz*

## RUTH

Meaning: *Friend, companion*
Appears: *Ruth; Matt. 1*
Ruth was a Gentile from Moab, east of the Dead Sea. She married a Jew, but when he died she traveled with her mother-in-law, Naomi, back to Naomi's hometown of Bethlehem. Although she was a foreigner, Ruth was accepted there. Following custom, one of Naomi's relatives, Boaz, married Ruth to make up for her loss. They became the great-grandparents of King David.

## THE FIERCE PHILISTINES

The Philistines were a warlike people who were long-term enemies of the Israelites, and who often defeated them in battle. On one occasion they captured the Ark of the Covenant, killing Eli's sons Hophni and Phineas.

*Philistine soldiers carry off the Ark*

**The Ark of the Covenant**
The Ark was a special decorated chest where the stone tablets of the law were kept. It was a sacred symbol of God's presence.

**Philistine warrior**
The Philistines had iron weapons before Israel, and were a constant threat. In the time of David, Israel gained the upper hand against them.

PHILISTINE HEAD
*A Philistine is shown in this Egyptian wall relief*

**Boaz** *first sees Ruth while inspecting his harvest*

## BOAZ

Meaning: *unknown*
Appears: *Ruth 2–4; Matt. 1; Luke 3*

Boaz was a wealthy Bethlehem farmer. When Naomi returned with her daughter-in-law Ruth, Boaz took pity on the two widows, and helped Ruth find food. Then Naomi realized he was a relative, so she petitioned Boaz to follow custom and marry Ruth in place of her dead husband. Boaz did so, with great joy.

## NAOMI

Meaning: *Pleasant*
Appears: *Ruth*

Naomi changed her name to Mara, meaning "bitter," because of her misfortune when her husband and two sons died. But Ruth loved her, went back to Bethlehem with her, and presented her with a beautiful grandson.

**Naomi** *plays with her grandson, Obed*

## ELI

Meaning: *Exalted*
Appears: *1 Sam. 1–4*

Eli was the priest at the chief shrine at Shiloh. Great festivals were held there with crowds of people traveling miles to attend. Eli's sons Hophni and Phineas were also priests there, but they exploited the visitors and acted wickedly. Eli was unable to stop them. Eventually they brought disaster on themselves and the whole family.

## HANNAH

Meaning: *Grace*
Appears: *1 Sam. 1, 2*

Every year Hannah, who was childless, went to Shiloh with her husband Elkanah. One year she prayed very hard and vowed that if she had a son, she would give him to God to serve at Shiloh. God gave her a son, Samuel, who became a temple servant from a very young age. Every year Hannah would bring him a new robe to wear. Hannah sang a beautiful song of thanksgiving.

SAMUEL AS A JUDGE
*This scene from a fresco by Santi Raffaello (1483–1520) shows Samuel anointing David with oil.*

## SAMUEL

Meaning: *God hears*
Appears: *1 Sam. 1–4, 7–13, 15, 16, 19, 25, 28*

Samuel was the last of the judges and also a prophet. God spoke to him vividly one night when he was still a boy, and many more times after that. When he was old, the Israelites asked Samuel to appoint a king for them and God led them to Saul. Samuel anointed him but later, when Saul's leadership failed, Samuel was led to Bethlehem where he anointed the young David.

### SEE ALSO

✝ Saul p 26
✝ David p 27
✝ Hophni and Phineas p 59

## ELIMELECH

Meaning: *My God is King*
Appears: *Ruth 1, 2, 4*

Elimelech was Naomi's husband. While living in Bethlehem, a famine forced them to move to the fertile lands of Moab. They settled there and one of their sons, Mahlon, married Ruth.

*God appears in a vision and tells* **Samuel** *that* **Eli** *will be punished*

# PROPHETS AND PRIESTS

THE CHIEF LEADERS of Israel were the kings, although the prophets and priests had great influence too. Because they conveyed messages directly from God, prophets could sometimes wield even more power than kings, especially when the kings had made mistakes. There were many prophets during Israel's history, and some have writings in the Bible. Priests were responsible for worship in the temple and also for teaching people how to obey God's laws.

*Elijah was fed by ravens during the drought*

## ABIATHAR

Meaning: *Father of excellence*
Appears: *1 Sam. 22, 23, 30; 2 Sam. 8, 15, 17, 19, 20; 1 Kings 1, 2; Mark 2*
Abiathar was King David's high priest. He joined David before he was made king, when Abiathar's family was massacred by Saul for helping David. When Absalom rebelled, Abiathar stayed in Jerusalem as a spy for David. He was later deposed by Solomon.

NATHAN THE PROPHET
*A late 15th-century manuscript of Nathan presenting* War, Plague, *and* Death *to King David.*

## ZADOK

Meaning: *Righteous*
Appears: *2 Sam. 8, 15, 17–20; 1 Kings 1, 2, 4; 1 Chron. 16, 24, 29*
Zadok was an assistant to Abiathar. He looked after the Ark of the Covenant when David brought it to Jerusalem, and he was later promoted by Solomon when Abiathar fell from favor. He anointed Solomon at a magnificent ceremony. Zadok's descendants were the chief priests of Israel for eight hundred years.

## NATHAN

Meaning: *God gave*
Appears: *2 Sam. 7, 12; 1 Kings 1*
Nathan was a prophet who, with Zadok, was responsible for crowning King Solomon. He had already served King David – first by giving him God's promise that his royal line would last forever, but later by denouncing him for his adultery with Bathsheba and his murder of her husband, Uriah. Nathan told David about a rich man who stole a poor man's pet lamb. When David got angry about this injustice, Nathan said "You are the man!"

## ELIJAH

Meaning: *The Lord is God*
Appears: *1 Kings 17–19, 21; 2 Kings 1, 2, 9, 10; Malachi 4; Matt. 11, 17; Luke 4; James 5*
Elijah was an awe-inspiring prophet before whom even wicked King Ahab quailed. When Ahab appointed prophets to worship Baal, Elijah told him that God would send no more rain. After three years of drought the people were starving, so Elijah staged a competition. He and the prophets of Baal prayed to their gods for fire to fall on an altar. When Elijah's altar burst into flames, the people turned back to God and the rain finally came.

## ELISHA

Meaning: *God is salvation*
Appears: *1 Kings 19; 2 Kings 2–9, 13; Luke 4*
Elisha was originally Elijah's servant, but before Elijah was taken to heaven in a chariot of fire he appointed Elisha to succeed him. During his life Elisha performed many miracles. One of the most famous concerned the son of a woman in Shunem. Elisha used to stay with her and her family, but one day her son fell ill and died. She laid him on Elisha's bed and sent for him. Elisha stretched himself on the boy's lifeless body, praying. Suddenly the boy sneezed seven times, and opened his eyes.

*Elisha brings the dead boy back to life*

## MICAIAH

Meaning: *Who is like the Lord?*
Appears: *1 Kings 22; 2 Chron. 18*

Micaiah bravely prophesied against King Ahab, when Ahab wanted to go to war with Syria. Ahab arranged for his own prophets to predict success. But then Micaiah, speaking for the Lord, predicted defeat and Ahab's death. Ahab refused to believe him and threw him in prison. But Micaiah's words came true and Ahab was killed in the ensuing battle.

## JONAH

Meaning: *Dove*
Appears: *2 Kings 14; Jonah; Matt. 12*

Jonah the prophet came from Gath-Hepher near Nazareth. God told him to go and prophesy in Nineveh, the capital of the Assyrian Empire. Jonah did not want God to forgive the Assyrians, so he sailed away in the opposite direction. God sent a storm to stop him, but Jonah knew why the storm had come, and told the sailors to throw him overboard. As soon as they did, the storm stopped and Jonah was swallowed by a large fish that later spat him out on the shore. Jonah then obeyed God, and went to preach in Nineveh. The Ninevites repented and God forgave them.

## THE SUFFERING OF JOB

Job was a wealthy but wise man. His book describes his suffering and how he tried to understand it in the light of his faith. Job lost everything in one day – his property and his family – then developed a terrible outbreak of boils. His friends said God was punishing him, but Job knew he had not wronged God. In the end he simply accepted God's wisdom and everything was returned to him.

*JOB'S FRIENDS*
*Eliphaz, Bildad, Zophar, and Elihu tried to help Job but only made life worse. This illustration shows Job with his friends.*

## AMOS

Meaning: *Burden bearer*
Appears: *Amos*

Amos was the first prophet whose words were written down. He came from Tekoa, near Bethlehem, and was a

*AMOS*

peasant farmer until God sent him to preach at the shrine in Bethel, where the rich families worshipped. The priests tried to stop Amos because he preached against injustice and predicted God's judgment on the king and his powerful supporters.

## HOSEA

Meaning: *Save, oh God!*
Appears: *Hosea*

Hosea was a prophet, in the northern kingdom, who preached about the pain God felt when people were unfaithful to him. By way of example, God told Hosea to marry a prostitute, who was then unfaithful to Hosea, who loved her. Hosea was then able to preach about God's feelings from his own experience.

## MICAH

Meaning: *Who is like the Lord?*
Appears: *Micah; Jer. 26*

Micah lived after Amos and Hosea, and preached in the southern kingdom of Judah. He spoke of the suffering and judgment that was coming on both the kingdoms, but also of the hope and restoration that God would bring. In particular he attacked the princes and false prophets for misleading the people, and looked forward to a time when God would send a special prince, to be born in Bethlehem.

*MICAH*

### SEE ALSO

✚ David p 27
✚ Absalom p 28
✚ Ahab p 30

*Jonah is swallowed by a great fish but survives*

*Huldah warns of disaster*

## HULDAH

Meaning: *Weasel*
Appears: *2 Kings 22; 2 Chron. 34*

Huldah was a female prophet, living at the same time as Jeremiah. When Hilkiah found God's law in the temple, he and a group of the king's officials went to consult Huldah. She told them that, because they had not been obeying the law, disaster would come – but not until after the time of Josiah who had been faithful to God. It is interesting that Hilkiah consulted Huldah, a female prophet, rather than Jeremiah.

to turn back to God because of the coming judgment. His words had little effect – especially on the kings who thought that Jeremiah was preaching treason when he said that Jerusalem would fall to the Babylonian army. King Zedekiah had Jeremiah thrown into a dark and muddy well. Eventually one of Zedekiah's servants persuaded the king to spare Jeremiah. Jeremiah lived through the final days of Jerusalem and was himself carried off to exile in Egypt.

*Jeremiah is lifted slowly out of the well*

## JEHOIADA

Meaning: *The Lord knows*
Appears: *2 Kings 11, 12; 2 Chron. 22–24*

Jehoiada was a famous chief priest of Jerusalem. He married King Ahaziah's sister but was horrified when her mother, Athaliah, seized the throne and tried to kill the entire royal family. Jehoiada and his wife stole Ahaziah's baby Joash and hid him for six years. Then they overthrew Athaliah and put Joash on the throne.

## URIAH

Meaning: *The Lord is my light*
Appears: *2 Kings 16; Isaiah 8*

Uriah was the high priest in Jerusalem during the reign of King Ahaz. When Ahaz went to Damascus, he saw a magnificent altar there. He made an exact plan and sent it to Uriah who had a copy made and installed in the Jerusalem temple.

**Hilkiah** *finds an important book*

## ISAIAH

Meaning: *The Lord has saved*
Appears: *2 Kings 19, 20; 2 Chron. 26, 32; Isaiah; and 22 verses in the New Testament*

Isaiah was a prophet in Judah, at the time of kings Ahaz and Hezekiah. His writings form the longest book in the Bible, although it may not all be his work. He had two sons: Shear-Jashub meaning "only a remnant shall return" and Maher-Shalal-Hashbaz which means "quick to the plunder, swift to the spoil."

## HILKIAH

Meaning: *The Lord is my portion*
Appears: *2 Kings 22, 23; 2 Chron. 34, 35*

Prompted by King Josiah, the high priest Hilkiah undertook a complete refurbishment of the temple. While cleaning up in preparation, he found a forgotten book of God's law.

## JEREMIAH

Meaning: *The Lord throws down*
Appears: *2 Chron. 35, 36; Jeremiah; Dan. 9; Matt. 2, 16, 27*

Jeremiah prophesied through the reigns of the last five kings of Judah, constantly warning people

## HABAKKUK

Meaning: *Embraced by God*
Appears: *Habakkuk*

It is not certain when Habakkuk was a prophet – probably around the time of Jeremiah. He was troubled by the Babylonian conquest of Judah. He knew that his people had been sinful, but he was aware that the Babylonians were even worse. He asked God how it could be just to use the Babylonians to bring judgment on his own people. God told Habakkuk to wait and have faith, and Habakkuk gladly agreed to trust in God.

## JOEL

*JOEL*

Meaning: *The Lord is God*

Appears: *Joel; Acts 2*

Joel prophesied just after a terrible swarm of locusts had devastated the land. He called the people to repent and trust in God's mercy and gave them God's promise that he would restore the land. On the day of Pentecost, Peter quoted Joel's prophecy of the gift of the Holy Spirit.

## EZEKIEL'S VISIONS

While Ezekiel was an exile in Babylon, he received visions from God who asked him to preach to his fellow exiles. Ezekiel told them that Jerusalem would be destroyed and his words came true.

*SCRIBES WROTE ON CLAY TABLETS*

**Clay tablets**

In one vision God told Ezekiel to draw Jerusalem under siege on a clay tablet to symbolize what was happening there.

**Dry bones**

Ezekiel saw a valley of dry human bones. God told him to call for the Spirit to blow on them, and gradually flesh and bones came to life. This vision represented the restoration of Israel.

*EZEKIEL*

*This page from the 12th-century Lambeth Bible depicts some of Ezekiel's visions.*

as God had prepared himself for the fall of Jerusalem. Ezekiel's prophecy is the third longest in the Bible, after Isaiah and Jeremiah.

*E FOR EZEKIEL*

*This decorative letter E is from a 12th-century Winchester Bible.*

## EZEKIEL

Meaning: *God strengthens*

Appears: *Ezekiel*

Ezekiel was a prophet and a priest. As a young priest he was carried off to exile in Babylon. Here God spoke to him and showed him visions to explain why the temple that he loved so much had been destroyed, and how it would one day be restored. God also told Ezekiel not to grieve after the death of his beloved wife but to prepare himself for this tragedy just

## JESHUA

Meaning: *The Lord is salvation*

Appears: *Ezra 3, 5, 8; Neh. 12; Haggai 1, 2; Zech. 3, 6*

After about fifty years in exile, King Cyrus of Persia allowed the leaders of the Jews to return to Jerusalem. Jeshua (also known as Joshua) went back as chief priest and re-established worship in the ruins of the temple. A few years later, Jeshua led the rebuilding of the temple.

*ZECHARIAH*

## ZECHARIAH

Meaning: *The Lord has remembered*

Appears: *Ezra 5, 6; Zechariah; Matt. 23*

Zechariah and Haggai both prophesied while the temple was being rebuilt in Jerusalem. Zechariah encouraged Jeshua the chief priest, and Zerubbabel the royal heir, not to give up but to carry on with the work.

*Jackals live in the land of Edom*

## MALACHI

Meaning: *My messenger*

Appears: *Malachi*

The prophecies of Malachi were probably the last to be included in the Old Testament. He criticized the Jews strongly for their apathetic attitude towards God. He also said that God would judge the land of Edom, making it a place fit only for wild jackals to live.

*Malachi appeals to his people*

### SEE ALSO

✝ Joash p 32

✝ Ahaz p 32

✝ Zerubbabel p 34

# THE FIRST ISRAELITE KINGS

WHEN THE Israelites became dissatisfied with the judges, and were also being subjected to renewed attacks from their old enemies the Philistines, the elders started to make demands for a king. The story of the first Israelite kings is told in the books of Samuel and 1 Kings. We hear about their greatness and their successes, but also their sins and failures.

*Saul leads his army to success against the Ammonites*

## SAUL

Meaning: *Asked*
Appears: *1 Sam. 9–11, 13–29, 31; 2 Sam. 1, 2; 1 Chron. 10*
Saul was the first king of Israel. He was tall and strong and started his reign well, under Samuel's guidance. When the Ammonite army attacked Jabesh-Gilead, the whole of Israel responded to Saul's call to fight. But then things began to go wrong. Saul came close to executing his son Jonathan and also started to disobey God. He became jealous of David and tried to murder him. Saul and Jonathan died together, fighting against the Philistines.

## JONATHAN

Meaning: *The Lord has given*
Appears: *1 Sam. 13, 14, 18–20, 23, 31; 2 Sam. 1*
Saul's oldest son Jonathan was a heroic warrior and should have become king after his father. Instead he was convinced that God would make his friend David king. When Saul was trying to kill David, Jonathan devised a way of warning David he was in danger by firing arrows a specified distance, while David hid nearby. When Jonathan died, David said "How are the mighty fallen."

*Jonathan lets David know he is in danger*

## ISHBOSHETH

Meaning: *Man of strength*
Appears: *2 Sam. 2–4*
Ishbosheth became king after his father Saul. His rule was not secure because the tribe of Judah had decided to follow David. Ishbosheth also depended on Abner, Saul's army commander, to keep him in power – but before long Abner decided to follow David, too.

## ABNER

Meaning: *Ner is my father*
Appears: *1 Sam. 14, 17, 20, 26; 2 Sam. 2–4; 1 Kings 2*
Abner was Saul's cousin and his army commander. He won many battles for Saul, and after Saul's death put Ishbosheth on the throne. He defended Ishbosheth against the followers of David; he also murdered Asahel, the brother of David's army commander.

## MEPHIBOSHETH

Meaning: *One who scatters strength*
Appears: *2 Sam. 4, 9, 16, 19, 21*
Mephibosheth, son of Jonathan, severely injured his feet in a childhood accident. Although disabled people were usually kept out of sight, David brought Mephibosheth to Jerusalem and treated him as one of his own sons.

## WITCH OF ENDOR

Meaning: *Witch from Endor*
Appears: *1 Sam. 28*
Although witchcraft was forbidden by God, many Israelites still practiced it in secret. When faced with the Philistine army, Saul was terrified because he thought God had left him. He went to the Witch of Endor who summoned the spirit of Samuel. He told Saul that God had given the kingdom to David and that he and his three sons would die in battle.

*THE WITCH OF ENDOR*
*This engraving by Schnorr von Carolsfeld (1794–1874) shows Saul at the Witch of Endor's where she has summoned the spirit of Samuel.*

*An elder pours oil from the anointing horn*

***David** is made king over Israel*

*BATHSHEBA*

## ABIGAIL

Meaning: *My father is joy*
Appears: *1 Sam. 25, 30; 2 Sam. 2, 3*

Abigail married David while he was on the run from Saul. Her first husband Nabal rudely insulted David. David was about to attack his household when Abigail intervened with a moving appeal.

this and David was truly sorry. Bathsheba became the mother of Solomon.

## BATHSHEBA

Meaning: *Daughter of abundance*
Appears: *2 Sam. 11, 12; 1 Kings 1, 2; 1 Chron. 3; Ps. 51*

Bathsheba was married to one of David's generals, Uriah, when David saw her bathing from his palace roof. He "arranged" Uriah's death in battle so he could marry her himself. Nathan the prophet denounced David for

## ABISHAG

Meaning: *My father is a nomad*
Appears: *1 Kings 1, 2*

Abishag was the last of David's wives. She was very beautiful, and he married her to keep him company in his old age.

### SEE ALSO

✝ The Philistines p 20
✝ Samuel p 21
✝ Nabal p 60

## DAVID

Meaning: *Beloved*
Appears: *1 Sam. 16 onward; and 893 verses throughout the Bible*

David is so special that no one else in the Bible has the same name. God sent Samuel to anoint David as the future king while he was still only a shepherd boy. David became famous when he fought the giant warrior Goliath. Saul was jealous of David and tried to kill him, but God protected him through many adventures and he became Israel's greatest king. The prophets thought of him as the forerunner of the Messiah.

## JESSE

Meaning: *unknown*
Appears: *Ruth 4; 1 Sam. 16, 17, 20, 22; 1 Chron 2; Isa. 11; Matt. 1; Rom. 15*

Jesse was the father of David – who was his eighth and youngest son. He also had two daughters. Jesse lived in Bethlehem where Samuel visited him to anoint one of his sons king. Jesse was amazed that David was God's choice.

## GOLIATH

Meaning: *Soothsayer*
Appears: *1 Sam. 17*

Goliath was a huge man – about 11 feet (3.3 meters) tall – descended from a tribe of giants called the Rephaim. Several such tribes lived in Canaan before Israel arrived. The Israelite spies said they felt like grasshoppers beside them. Goliath wore full armor and carried an enormous spear. He challenged Saul's army to single combat, but no one except David was willing to take him on.

***Michal** helps David escape*

## MICHAL

Meaning: *Who is like God?*
Appears: *1 Sam. 14, 18, 19, 25; 2 Sam. 3, 6*

Saul promised his younger daughter Michal in marriage to whoever killed Goliath. This greatly pleased Michal because she had fallen in love with David. Later, when she knew Saul's soldiers were coming to kill David, she helped him escape through a window.

## DAVID AND GOLIATH

David's defeat of Goliath is one of the most famous stories in the Bible. The young shepherd killed Goliath with a single shot from his sling, and the whole Philistine army fled in fear.

*SLING SHOT*
*The sling was a common weapon in ancient times*

**Expert shot**
David used his sling to protect Jesse's sheep from wild animals. By the time he met Goliath, he was already an expert shot.

**Goliath loses his head**
David cut off Goliath's head using the giant's own massive sword, then carried it in triumph to Saul. David's victory was proof that God could deliver Israel from any enemy.

*DAVID BEHEADS GOLIATH*
*This painting is by Michiel Coxie (1499–1592).*

*Amnon is killed for the rape of Tamar*

## AMNON

Meaning: *Faithful*
Appears: *2 Sam. 3, 13*
Amnon was David's oldest son. His story shows how David's family started to fall apart after David's adultery with Bathsheba. Amnon fell in love with his half-sister Tamar, but raped her. Absalom, Tamar's brother, waited two years then murdered him.

## TAMAR

Meaning: *Palm tree*
Appears: *2 Sam. 13*
Tamar was David's daughter by his wife Maacah. She was tricked by her half-brother Amnon who asked her to cook for him. When she went to serve the food, he raped her. Tamar was devastated and lived in seclusion at her brother's.

*Absalom gets his hair caught in the branches of a tree*

## ABSALOM

Meaning: *Father of peace*
Appears: *2 Sam. 3, 13–19*
Absalom was David's third son. After he killed Amnon, David banished him from the kingdom. Three years later he came back and started to plan a rebellion against his father. He made himself popular with the people and won their hearts. After four years Absalom made himself king and David had to flee from Jerusalem. A battle followed, during which Absalom was killed after his mule went under a tree and his long hair got caught in the branches. Though Absalom had done him much harm, David mourned him.

## SHEBA

Meaning: *Seven*
Appears: *2 Sam. 20*
Sheba was a Benjaminite who also led a rebellion against David. Relationships between Judah and the other tribes had always been tense. David, who belonged to Judah, worked hard to keep the tribes together. But Sheba urged some tribes to break away and attack him. They were unsuccessful and Sheba was beheaded.

## ADONIJAH

Meaning: *The Lord is my God*
Appears: *2 Sam. 3; 1 Kings 1, 2*
Adonijah was David's fourth son. When David was old, Adonijah tried to seize the throne with the support of Joab and Abiathar the high priest. David remained determined that Solomon should be king.

*ADONIJAH*

## JOAB

Meaning: *The Lord God is father*
Appears: *2 Sam. 2, 3, 10–12, 14, 17–20, 23–24; 1 Kings 1, 2, 11*
Joab was David's nephew and also the commander of his army. He was not intimidated by David and often spoke sharply to him. He could be cruel and jealous, and committed three murders: of Abner, of Absalom, as he hung in the tree, and of his cousin Amasa.

## ABISHAI

Meaning: *Father of giving*
Appears: *1 Sam. 26; 2 Sam. 2, 3, 10, 16, 18–21, 23*
Abishai was the brother of Joab and they had both known David from his outlaw days. Abishai had many adventures with David, including creeping into Saul's camp at night and stealing Saul's spear. He shared the army command with Joab and was chief of David's private guard.

## AMASA

Meaning: *Bearer of burdens*
Appears: *2 Sam. 17, 19, 20; 1 Kings 2*
Amasa was David's nephew, the son of his sister Abigail. When Absalom rebelled against David, he appointed his cousin Amasa to command his army. Amasa was defeated by Joab, but then David surprised everyone by sacking Joab and appointing Amasa. He hoped to win over the people who had fought for Absalom. But Joab killed Amasa in a brutal way.

## BENAIAH

Meaning: *The Lord has built up*
Appears: *2 Sam. 8, 20, 23; 1 Kings 1, 2, 4; 1 Chron. 11, 27*
Benaiah, son of Jehoiada, was one of David's "mighty men." David surrounded himself with skilled fighters and commanders, and Benaiah was in charge of the band of foreign fighters who acted as David's personal police force. He became the supreme commander under Solomon, replacing Joab. Solomon ordered Benaiah to kill Joab, because he had supported Adonijah's attempt to take the throne. Joab took refuge in the temple, but Benaiah followed and killed him.

## SOLOMON

Meaning: *Peaceful*
Appears: *2 Sam. 12; 1 Kings 1–11; and 237 verses in the Bible*

Solomon was David's son who reigned after him in Jerusalem for forty years. At his birth the prophet Nathan gave him another name – Jedidiah, meaning "loved by the Lord." In many ways his life reflected the meaning of both his names. His rule was peaceful and, as a result, Solomon became very wealthy. He built several palaces for himself and his household (including three hundred wives). His biggest project was the temple in Jerusalem, which was built by thirty thousand laborers over a period of seven years. Solomon was famous for his wisdom, and some of his sayings are in the books of Proverbs and Ecclesiastes.

*Skilled workers decorate the stone*

*Solomon oversees the work on the new temple in Jerusalem*

## HIRAM

Meaning: *My brother is exalted*
Appears: *1 Kings 7; 2 Chron. 4*

Hiram's mother was an Israelite from Naphtali. Her son, also called Huram-abi, was the chief designer who worked on Solomon's Temple. Many materials for the temple came from King Hiram of Tyre. Hiram was a skilled metalworker; he fashioned bronze pillars for the front of the temple and a huge bath for holy water that rested on twelve bronze bulls. He also made many intricate decorations. When the temple was finished it was dedicated by Solomon in a magnificent ceremony.

### SEE ALSO

✝ King Hiram p 17
✝ Nathan p 22
✝ David p 27

## QUEEN OF SHEBA

Meaning: *Queen from Sheba*
Appears: *1 Kings 10; 2 Chron. 9*

This queen ruled in an area of modern-day Yemen. When news of Solomon's wealth and wisdom reached her, she decided to make the long journey to meet him. She arrived with a caravan of camels bearing gold, spices, and precious stones, and asked Solomon all the difficult questions she could think of. After hearing his answers and seeing his palace, she said, "Not even half was told me! In wisdom and wealth you have far exceeded the report I heard. Praise be to the Lord your God, who delighted in you and placed you on the throne of Israel."

*The Queen of Sheba travels along a trade route to visit Solomon*

## SOLOMON'S WISDOM

When Solomon asked God for wisdom and knowledge to rule the people of Israel, his request was granted. God also promised Solomon riches and honor surpassing those of other kings.

**Solomon's mine**
Under Solomon's rule Israel grew rich. Solomon ran a huge quarry where stone was mined to build the new temple. Many thousands of captives worked in the mines.

*SITE OF SOLOMON'S MINES*

**Solomon's wisdom**
Two prostitutes had baby boys. When one died, his mother secretly swapped the babies. To decide the real mother, Solomon told a soldier to cut the living baby in two. The guilty woman agreed, but the real mother was horrified.

# KINGS OF ISRAEL

WHEN SOLOMON died, it was no longer possible to hold the kingdom together. The southern tribes of Judah and Benjamin, which included Jerusalem in their territory, remained loyal to David's family, while the northern tribes broke away under the leadership of Jeroboam. The northern kingdom came to be known as Israel and the southern as Judah. Sadly, the northern kingdom abandoned God in favor of idolatry.

When **Jeroboam** tries to arrest the man of God his hand shrivels up

desires. One story tells how he sulked because Naboth would not sell him his vineyard. Jezebel wrote letters in Ahab's name so that Naboth was falsely accused of blasphemy and stoned to death. She then took his vineyard for Ahab. Elijah the prophet met Ahab there, and told him that he would also die violently like Naboth.

## JEZEBEL
Meaning: *unknown*
Appears: *1 Kings 16, 18, 19, 21; 2 Kings 9*
The wife of Ahab, Jezebel was a passionate devotee of the Baal god called Melqart, and brought hundreds of his priests with her to Samaria. She also persuaded Ahab to worship Baal. Jezebel was eventually killed by Jehu.

**Ahab** wants to buy Naboth's vineyard to use as a vegetable garden

## AHAZIAH
Meaning: *The Lord has grasped me*
Appears: *1 Kings 22; 2 Kings 1*
Ahaziah was Ahab's son. His reign only lasted for two years because he fell down a stairwell and seriously injured himself. He carried on his father and mother's devotion to Baal and sent messengers to ask the Baal god of Ekron (one of the Philistine towns) if he would recover from his fall. God sent the prophet Elijah to intervene but Ahaziah refused to listen and died.

## JEROBOAM
Meaning: *May the people increase*
Appears: *1 Kings 11–14*
Jeroboam was the first ruler of the northern kingdom. He was a gifted young officer in Solomon's service when Ahijah told him that God intended to give him ten of the twelve tribes to rule. His family would also reign forever if Jeroboam remained faithful to God. Sadly, when Jeroboam came to power he worshipped idols. Although a prophet came to denounce him, and even made his hand shrivel up, Jeroboam would not change his ways.

## OMRI
Meaning: *Worshipper of God*
Appears: *1 Kings 16*
Omri was the army commander when he seized the throne from Jeroboam and reigned for twelve years. He built a new capital city at Samaria, but under his rule the people became less faithful to God than before.

## AHAB
Meaning: *God is father*
Appears: *1 Kings 16–22*
Ahab inherited the throne of Israel from his father Omri. He was a weak king, dominated by his wife Jezebel and full of selfish

## JORAM
Meaning: *The Lord is exalted*
Appears: *2 Kings 1, 3, 8, 9*
Ahaziah's brother Joram succeeded to the throne because Ahaziah had no children to take over. Joram reigned for twelve years, but fared no better than Ahab or Ahaziah because his mother Jezebel was still alive and a bad influence. Joram was eventually murdered by Jehu who then proclaimed himself king.

JEZEBEL

## JEHU

Meaning: *unknown*
Appears: *1 Kings 19; 2 Kings 9, 10*

Like Jeroboam, and David before him, Jehu was appointed king by a prophet while another king (Joram) was still on the throne. But unlike David, Jehu did not wait for Joram to die. As soon as he received the message, he murdered Joram and all the male heirs of Ahab (seventy men in all). Then he decided to bring an end to Baal worship. He tricked the prophets and priests of Baal into going into their temple together, then killed them all.

*KING JEHU Jehu bows before King Shalmaneser III on this stone monument from Assyria*

*JEHOASH*

## JEHOASH

Meaning: *The Lord has given*
Appears: *1 Kings 11, 12; 2 Kings 13, 14*

Jehoash was the grandson of Jehu. When Elisha the prophet was a very old man, he sent for Jehoash and gave him special power to defeat the Syrians, who had been oppressing Israel. Jehoash was able to win back the land lost to the Syrians. Sadly, Jehoash went to war against Judah. He destroyed part of the wall of Jerusalem and stole from the temple.

## JEROBOAM II

Meaning: *May the people increase*
Appears: *2 Kings 14; Amos 7*

The Bible tells us very little about Jeroboam II, son of Jehoash, who reigned for forty years. This is because he was just as wicked as his predecessors, encouraging the worship of Baal. Amos prophesied against his rule and accused him of injustice to the poor. Yet Jeroboam was a very successful king who extended the borders of Israel and attracted great wealth into the country. During his long rule there was peace and prosperity.

## ZECHARIAH

Meaning: *The Lord has remembered*
Appears: *2 Kings 14, 15*

Zechariah, the son of Jeroboam II, reigned for only six months. At this time the power of the great empire of Assyria was beginning to grow, and the peace and prosperity of Jeroboam's reign was coming to an end. Zechariah was the first of a series of kings who reigned for only a short time. He was assassinated by Shallum, who reigned for one month before being killed by Menahem.

## PEKAH

Meaning: *Opening*
Appears: *2 Kings 15, 16; Isa. 7*

While Pekah was king of Israel he tried to resist the power of Assyria by creating an alliance with Syria. In an attempt to increase his power, Pekah then attacked Judah. At the end of Pekah's reign, the king of Assyria invaded Israel and occupied more than half the land. In the confusion Pekah was murdered by Hoshea.

## HOSHEA

Meaning: *Let the Lord save!*
Appears: *2 Kings 15, 17*

Hoshea was the last king of Israel. After he had seized the throne from Pekah, he began paying tribute to the Assyrian king, Shalmaneser. He stopped when he wanted help against Assyria from the Egyptians. However, after a long seige, Samaria was captured by the Assyrians and Hoshea was taken into exile with thousands of Israelites.

### SEE ALSO

✝ Amos p 23
✝ Ahijah p 58

## JEROBOAM AND THE DIVIDED KINGDOM

Jeroboam set the course of two hundred years of history when he introduced Baal worship alongside the worship of the Lord. The Bible makes it clear that this was why the northern kingdom ceased to exist.

*JEROBOAM'S IDOLATRY Jeroboam worships a golden calf; painting by Jean-Honoré Fragonard (1732–1806).*

**Jeroboam**
Jeroboam created two new shrines (worship centers) at Dan and Bethel so that people would not need to go to Jerusalem to worship. These shrines were not dedicated to the worship of God but to two golden calves.

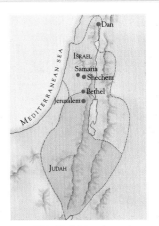

**Divided kingdom**
The map shows Israel, with its chief cities, and Judah with its capital of Jerusalem.

# KINGS OF JUDAH

IN THE SOUTHERN KINGDOM of Judah, the descendants of David continued to rule. These kings remained more faithful to God than those in the northern kingdom and, for a while, life was more peaceful. But it did not last. The kingdom existed for three hundred and fifty years until the Babylonians took over and destroyed Solomon's beautiful temple.

*Rehoboam ignores the elders who advise him to bring an end to forced labor*

## REHOBOAM

Meaning: *Expansion of the people*
Appears: *1 Kings 11, 12, 14; 2 Chron. 10–13*
Rehoboam was the last ruler of a united kingdom. When Solomon died, people pleaded for an end to forced labor. Rehoboam listened to his young advisers and made the work harder. This led to a rebellion that finally split the kingdom in two leaving Rehoboam with Judah and Benjamin. After five years the Egyptian army invaded Judah and took the treasures from the temple.

people. Because he wanted to be friendly with Israel, he persuaded his son Jehoram to marry Athaliah. This proved to be a big mistake.

*QUEEN ATHALIAH*

## ATHALIAH

Meaning: *The Lord is exalted*
Appears: *2 Kings 8, 11; 2 Chron. 22–24*
Athaliah was the daughter of King Ahab and Jezebel. Athaliah corrupted her husband Jehoram and her son Ahaziah, both of whom reigned briefly in Jerusalem. When Ahaziah died, Athaliah seized the throne and killed the whole royal family – or so she thought. Her grandson Joash had been hidden in the temple.

## JOASH

Meaning: *God supports*
Appears: *2 Kings 11, 12; 2 Chron. 24*
Joash became king of Judah at the age of seven when Jehoiada brought him out of hiding in the temple. When wicked Queen Athaliah heard the people cheering she rushed into the temple shouting "Treason! Treason!," but Jehoiada had her killed. While Joash was king he repaired and re-equipped the temple.

## ASA

Meaning: *God heals*
Appears: *1 Kings 15, 16; 2 Chron. 14–16*
Asa, grandson of Rehoboam, reigned for forty-one years. He campaigned to remove idols and pagan influences from the land and restored the gold and silver to the temple. When the Egyptians invaded again, Asa trusted God to help him and defeated their huge army.

## JEHOSHAPHAT

Meaning: *The Lord is the judge*
Appears: *1 Kings 15, 22; 2 Kings 3; 2 Chron. 17–21*
Jehoshaphat, Asa's son, also stayed faithful to God. He built forts to protect Judah and sent a team of Levites to teach God's law to the

## AMAZIAH

Meaning: *The Lord is mighty*
Appears: *2 Kings 13, 14; 2 Chron. 24, 25*
Amaziah was a good king who recaptured some of the territory that had been lost to the king of Edom. Disaster struck when he decided to go to war against King Jehoash of Israel. Amaziah's army was defeated, the temple was plundered, and part of Jerusalem was destroyed.

## AHAZ

Meaning: *He has grasped*
Appears: *2 Kings 16; 2 Chron. 28, Isaiah 7*
Under Ahaz, life in Judah began to go seriously wrong. Ahaz started worshipping idols and sacrificed his children to them. When he set up a pagan altar in the temple, God brought an army against Judah – a joint force from Israel and Syria. Isaiah the prophet appealed to Ahaz to trust in God for help, but Ahaz preferred to send messengers to the king of Assyria. The result was defeat by the invaders and submission to Assyria for the next hundred years.

*King Ahaz worships at a pagan altar*

*Hezekiah* prays to God to save him from death

*Isaiah* says God will heal you

## HEZEKIAH

Meaning: *The Lord is my strength*
Appears: *2 Kings 18–20; 2 Chron. 29–32; Isa. 36–39; Jer. 26*

Unlike his father Ahaz, Hezekiah was true to God. He restored worship in the temple and held a Passover festival with people from the north. While he was king, the Assyrians attacked Judah. Hezekiah prayed hard and the Assyrian army was struck down by disease.

## AMON

Meaning: *Reliable, truthful*
Appears: *2 Kings 21; 2 Chron. 33*

Amon, son of Manasseh, turned his back on God and did not hesitate to start worshipping the Assyrian idols again. He was killed by a group of his own officers who wanted the throne for themselves. Eventually these plotters were murdered and Amon's son became king.

## JOSIAH AND THE BOOK OF THE LAW

Deuteronomy is probably the book that Hilkiah found in the temple. It teaches that God will bless the Israelites if they obey his law but banish them from their land if they worship idols. It also advises that sacrifices and festivals must be held at one central temple. Josiah realized that Israelite land would be lost unless he closed all shrines except the temple in Jerusalem.

*Josiah* reads from the book and renews his promise to God

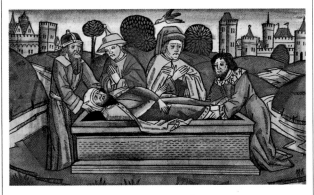

## MANASSEH

Meaning: *Making to forget*
Appears: *2 Kings 21; 2 Chron. 33*

Hezekiah's son Manasseh reverted to the bad ways of his grandfather Ahaz. He started worshipping pagan gods and even sacrificed his son to the Ammonite god Molech. Disaster followed. Manasseh was taken prisoner to Babylon where he repented. He tried to put things right, but it was too late and he died a sad man.

*JOSIAH IS LAID TO REST*
This illustration is from the 15th-century Nuremberg Bible.

## JOSIAH

Meaning: *May the Lord give*
Appears: *1 Kings 13; 2 Kings 22, 23; 2 Chron. 34, 35*

Josiah was only eight when he became king. He wanted to return to the one true God, and with the power of Assyria waning, this became easier. When Hilkiah the high priest found a book of God's law, lost during the reigns of Manasseh and Amon, Josiah realized that God was angry because of his father's and grandfather's lack of faith. He consulted the prophetess Huldah who confirmed that God's judgment was coming. Josiah started reforming the country, but it was too late.

## ZEDEKIAH

Meaning: *The Lord is righteousness*
Appears: *2 Kings 24, 25; 2 Chron. 36; Jer. 21, 32, 34, 37–39, 52*

The last king of Judah was Zedekiah. Because Josiah had repented, God promised that disaster would not fall until after his death. His sons Jehoiakim and Zedekiah both ruled Judah but did not follow their father's wise ways. They did not care about God and rebelled against King Nebuchadnezzar of Babylon, who was the ruling power in the region. Nebuchadnezzar destroyed Jerusalem and the temple, killed Zedekiah's sons, then blinded him. The country was in total ruin.

### SEE ALSO

✝ Huldah p 24
✝ Jehoiada p 24
✝ Jehoram p 60

*Zedekiah* and his people are taken into captivity in Babylon

# JEWISH NATION IN EXILE

AND SO IT HAPPENED. As Josiah had feared, and Jeremiah had predicted, disaster fell upon Judah as well as Israel, and the whole nation was exiled from the promised land. Although the Israelites suffered under the rule of various foreign kings, within fifty years they began to return with great hope and joy.

*Only **Daniel** is able to read the strange writing*

## DANIEL
Meaning: *God is my judge*
Appears: *Daniel*
Daniel and his friends were taken to Babylon as captives in 605 BC, and trained to work for Nebuchadnezzar. Daniel was renamed Belteshazzar, after a Babylonian god Bel, even though he only ever worshipped God. Daniel had a special gift that allowed him to understand the meaning of dreams. On two occasions he was able to interpret Nebuchadnezzar's extraordinary dreams. He was also able to read the writing that appeared on the wall during Belshazzar's feast. God kept Daniel safe through many adventures, especially when King Darius threw him in the lions' den.

## SHADRACH
Meaning: *Command of Aku*
Appears: *Dan. 1, 2, 3*
Like his friend Daniel, Shadrach also lost his real name in Babylon. He was originally Hananiah, meaning "the Lord is gracious." He certainly experienced the grace of God when he was saved from the blazing furnace.

## MESHACH
Meaning: *Who is what Aku is?*
Appears: *Dan. 1, 2, 3*
Another of Daniel's friends, Meshach's real name was Mishael, meaning "who is what God is?" When Meshach, Shadrach, and Abednego refused to worship a pagan idol, Nebuchadnezzar decided to burn them.

## ABEDNEGO
Meaning: *Servant of Nego*
Appears: *Dan. 1, 2, 3*
The third of Daniel's friends, Abednego's old name was Azariah, meaning "the Lord helps me." God was able to help Abednego when he refused to worship a huge golden idol that King Nebuchadnezzar had set up.

## JEHOIACHIN
Meaning: *The Lord will establish*
Appears: *2 Kings 24, 25; 2 Chron. 36; Esther 2; Jer. 24, 27, 52*
As a young man, Jehoiachin reigned for just three months before being carried away to Babylon where he was imprisoned for thirty-seven years. When Nebuchadnezzar died, his successor Evil-Merodach released him and gave him an allowance.

## ZERUBBABEL
Meaning: *Seed of Babylon*
Appears: *Ezra 2–5; Neh. 7, 12; Haggai 1, 2; Zech. 4*
Zerubbabel, Jehoiachin's grandson, was born in Babylon but knew that he was destined to become king in Jerusalem. As soon as it was possible, he returned to Judah and, with help, set about restoring the kingdom. His first task was to rebuild the temple.

## HAGGAI
Meaning: *unknown*
Appears: *Ezra 5, 6; Haggai*
Haggai the prophet came to Jerusalem in 520 BC. At this time, the work of rebuilding the temple had come to a standstill. Haggai preached inspiringly about it, and within four years Zerubbabel and Jeshua the priest completed the task.

## EZRA
Meaning: *God is a help*
Appears: *Ezra 7, 10; Neh. 8*
When Ezra, a priest, was sent back to Jerusalem by King Artaxerxes of Persia, he was horrified that Jews in Jerusalem had intermarried with the surrounding tribes. He immediately made them divorce their pagan wives.

*Shadrach, Meshach, and **Abednego** are told they will be thrown into a fiery furnace*

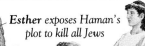

*Esther exposes Haman's plot to kill all Jews*

**Haman**

## ESTHER

Meaning: *Star*

Appears: *Esther*

Esther was a beautiful Jewish woman who lived in Persia under the rule of Xerxes. She became Xerxes' queen and was able to prevent a dreadful plan to get rid of all the Jews in the vast Persian empire. She kept her Jewish identity and name Hadassah (meaning "myrtle") a secret until she was able to use it to save her people.

## MORDECAI

Meaning: *Named after Marduk, the Babylonian god.*

Appears: *Esther*

Mordecai was Esther's uncle. She became queen while he was a minor official in King Xerxes' palace. He foiled a plot against the king's life, which earned him Xerxes' gratitude. When he heard about Haman's plot to exterminate the Jews, he told Esther and encouraged her to plead with Xerxes. "Who knows but that you have come to royal position for such a time as this?" he said.

*Mordecai overhears a plot to assassinate Xerxes*

## VASHTI

Meaning: *One who is desired*

Appears: *Esther 1–2*

Vashti was the queen of King Xerxes (who was called Ahasuerus in the Bible). On the seventh day of a special feast, Xerxes summoned Vashti to show off her beauty to his guests. She refused. He was so furious that he deposed her and decided to choose another queen. Esther was his choice.

## HAMAN

Meaning: *unknown*

Appears: *Esther 3–9*

Haman, Xerxes' chief minister, hated the Jews because Mordecai would not bow down to him. He persuaded Xerxes to sign an order to kill all Jews in the Persian Empire. Esther asked Haman and the king to eat with her and then identified Haman as the murderer of her people. Haman was hanged on the gallows that he had built for Mordecai.

*HAMAN*

## NEHEMIAH

Meaning: *The Lord comforts*

Appears: *Nehemiah*

Nehemiah was a brilliant administrator and man of action. He served King Artaxerxes of Persia, and in 445 BC obtained permission to return to

*Nehemiah goes at night to inspect the city walls*

Jerusalem to rebuild the city wall. He inspired the people with his vision and, against great opposition, completed the project. He was sustained by his complete faith in God.

## SANBALLAT

Meaning: *Sin (the moon god) has given life*

Appears: *Neh. 2, 4, 6, 13*

When Artaxerxes appointed Nehemiah as governor of Judah, Sanballat felt insulted. He objected to Nehemiah rebuilding Jerusalem and plotted, unsuccessfully, to kill him.

### SEE ALSO

✝ Nebuchadnezzar p 36
✝ Belshazzar p 37
✝ Xerxes p 37

## DANIEL IN THE LIONS' DEN

Daniel's relationship with the king aroused much jealousy among his enemies. They persuaded King Darius that anyone who did not worship him should be thrown in the lions' den. When Daniel was found praying to God, Darius reluctantly agreed to punish him. In the night an angel from God came and shut the lions' mouths.

*Daniel prays to God for help and the lions do not harm him*

# FOREIGN KINGS

THE ANCIENT WORLD was dominated by superpowers, like the world today. The location of Palestine meant that the Israelites were surrounded – by Egyptians to the south, and by Assyrians and Babylonians to the north and east. These were mighty empires with huge armies, so Israel was constantly under threat and needed to trust in God. Israelite kings are often mentioned in ancient records that have been found by archaeologists.

## SHISHAK

Meaning: *unknown*
Appears: *1 Kings 11, 14; 2 Chron. 12*
Shishak was the Egyptian pharaoh, or king, from 945–924 BC. Although he allowed Jeroboam to hide from Solomon in Egypt, he later invaded Judah and took all the gold from the temple.

## NECO

Meaning: *unknown*
Appears: *2 Kings 23; 2 Chron. 35, 36; Jer. 46*
When the Assyrian Empire collapsed, Neco tried to take Palestine before Babylon. Josiah was killed in 609 BC when Neco's army marched against the Babylonians.

*PHARAOH NECO*

*The wise men cannot interpret the king's dream*

## BEN-HADAD

Meaning: *Son of the god Hadad*
Appears: *1 Kings 15, 20; 2 Kings 6, 8, 13*
Two Ben-Hadads appear in the Bible – both kings of Syria. The first fought King Ahab, while the second (his grandson) fought Jehoash.

## HAZAEL

Meaning: *God has seen*
Appears: *1 Kings 19; 2 Kings 8, 9, 10, 12, 13*
When Elisha told Hazael he would become king of Syria, Hazael killed Ben-Hadad I and took the throne. Under his rule Syria grew in power and captured parts of Israel.

## TIGLATH-PILESER III

Meaning: *My trust is in the son of Esarra*
Appears: *2 Kings 15, 16; 1 Chron. 5*
Tiglath-Pileser III helped to expand the Assyrian Empire. In 732 BC his army captured Damascus, sending waves of terror through Israel and Judah. King Ahaz tried to join forces with him but became his servant.

## SHALMANESER

Meaning: *Sulmanu is leader*
Appears: *2 Kings 17, 18*
Shalmaneser was the mighty king of Assyria who put King Hoshea in prison. Shalmaneser besieged Samaria for three years until it finally fell.

## SENNACHERIB

Meaning: *May the god Sin replace the (lost) brothers*
Appears: *2 Kings 18, 19; 2 Chron. 32; Isa. 36, 37*
Sennacherib was the son of Sargon II, who had captured Samaria and greatly strengthened the empire. Sennacherib tried to capture

*KING SENNACHERIB*

Jerusalem in 700 BC. Poor King Hezekiah was helpless in the face of Sennacherib's mighty army, but he prayed to God and the city was miraculously saved.

*Nebuchadnezzar has a strange dream*

## NEBUCHADNEZZAR

Meaning: *May the god Nabu protect my boundary-stone*
Appears: *2 Kings 24, 25; 2 Chron. 36; Jer. 21, 22, 24, 25, 27–29, 39, 43, 46, 52; Dan. 1–5*
Nebuchadnezzar's father, Nabopolassar, brought about the collapse of the Assyrian Empire in 612 BC. When Nebuchadnezzar came to the throne he spent the first years of his long reign bringing the various parts of the Assyrian empire – including Judah – under his control. Over the years he carried leading Jews into exile, finally destroying Jerusalem with great brutality. He was troubled by dreams that baffled all his wise men except Daniel.

## THE PALACE OF KING NEBUCHADNEZZAR

Nebuchadnezzar was enormously wealthy because he used his army to collect taxes from all his subjects. He built huge temples in Babylon and a vast palace for himself. His famous "hanging gardens" became one of the wonders of the ancient world.

### Nebuchadnezzar

Daniel tells us that one day Nebuchadnezzar boasted of the magnificent city he had built. In anger, God took it all away from him – until the king was willing to acknowledge that God is the source of all power.

*NEBUCHADNEZZAR WITH DANIEL*
*The king questions Daniel: painting by the Master of Marradi c.1480.*

### The Ishtar Gate

Ishtar was the fertility goddess of Babylon. The gate to her temple, covered in a mosaic of colored stones, showed images of dragons and bulls.

*PART OF THE ISHTAR GATE*

## BELSHAZZAR

Meaning: *May the god Bel protect the king*
Appears: *Dan. 5*

Belshazzar was a prince who reigned with Nabonidus, the last king of Babylon. Belshazzar held a feast and used goblets from the temple in Jerusalem to honor other gods. A hand appeared, writing on the wall and announcing his downfall, which soon followed.

## CYRUS THE GREAT

Meaning: *unknown*
Appears: *2 Chron. 36; Ezra 1, 3–6; Isa. 44, 45; Dan. 1, 6, 10*

Cyrus, king of Persia, slowly defeated the nations around him. In 539 BC he captured Babylon and became "king of the world." Then he freed all captives, including the Jews whom he sent back to Jerusalem. Ezra records the decree that Cyrus issued, giving them permission to rebuild their temple.

*KING CYRUS*
*A 14th-century book illustration shows Cyrus's brutal death.*

## DARIUS I

Meaning: *He who upholds the good*
Appears: *Ezra 4–6; Dan. 5, 6; Hag. 1; Zech. 1*

Darius ruled the mighty Persian Empire, which stretched from Europe to India, from 522–486 BC. When enemies of the Jews in Judah tried to stop the rebuilding of the temple, Darius wrote a letter telling them to help the Jews, and to provide supplies – on pain of death. The Greeks defeated his army at the battle of Marathon (490 BC).

## XERXES

Meaning: *unknown*
Appears: *Ezra 4; Esther*

Xerxes succeeded his father Darius and ruled from 486–465 BC. He tried to take Greece, but was defeated at the battle of Salamis in 480 BC. He chose Esther to be his queen, and changed

*King Darius has officials who administer his empire*

## ARTAXERXES

Meaning: *Kingdom of righteousness*
Appears: *Ezra 4, 6–8; Neh. 2, 5, 13*

Artaxerxes was the son of Xerxes and ruled the Persian Empire from 465–425 BC. He allowed his cup-bearer Nehemiah to return to Jerusalem in 445 BC to help with the rebuilding work there. He also allowed Ezra the scribe to go, and Ezra records the long letter of permission which Artaxerxes gave him.

*Artaxerxes listens to his cup-bearer who tells him that Jerusalem lies in ruins*

his mind about killing the Jews when he discovered she was Jewish. The book of Esther shows the power he had over his subjects.

## SEE ALSO

✝ Ahab p 30
✝ Josiah p 33
✝ Daniel p 34
✝ Esther p 35

# PEOPLE OF THE NEW TESTAMENT

THE RESURRECTION OF JESUS
*The figure of Christ is the focus of this 18th-century Greek icon.*

THE NEW TESTAMENT centers around Jesus, who Christians regard as the Messiah – the "son of David" whose arrival was foretold by the prophets of the Old Testament. At the time of Jesus' birth, many Jews were waiting for these prophecies to be fulfilled, and for Israel to be restored to its former glory. The New Testament tells the amazing story of Jesus and his disciples; how they came to believe in him and began to spread his message, first among their fellow Jews, then more widely. The New Testament also tells of those who opposed the new faith, and the struggle of the early church to establish Christianity.

## MAIN EVENTS IN JESUS' LIFE

Jesus lived for only thirty-three years yet his teaching has changed the way we think and lead our lives. The four Gospels, written by Matthew, Mark, Luke, and John, give a clear picture of Jesus' life, death, and resurrection.

### JESUS' BIRTH AND CHILDHOOD

• Jesus is born in a stable in Bethlehem in about 4 BC.
• Angels announce the birth of the Lord to shepherds.
• King Herod plans to kill Jesus, so Joseph and Mary take him to Egypt.
• After Herod's death, they return to Nazareth where Jesus grows up.
• Aged twelve, Jesus goes to Jerusalem for Passover. He talks to teachers in the temple.

*Jesus' parents find him in the temple*

### THE BEGINNING OF JESUS' MINISTRY

• Aged about thirty, Jesus is baptized by John the Baptist and the Holy Spirit descends on him like a dove.
• Before teaching, Jesus goes to the desert for forty days and is tempted by the devil.
• He then returns to Judea, and preaches: "Repent, for the Kingdom of God is near!"

*Jesus is tempted in the desert*

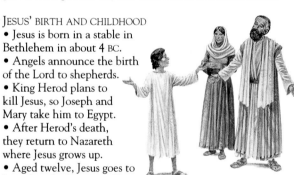

### THE NEXT THREE YEARS

• Throughout Galilee, Samaria, and Judea, Jesus preaches and heals the sick.
• He chooses a special group of twelve disciples to carry on his work after he dies.
• Jesus performs many miracles, such as feeding a vast crowd with just five loaves and two fish.
• He teaches people that they should love their enemies.

*Jesus feeds five thousand people*

### JESUS' LAST WEEK

• People cheer as Jesus rides into Jerusalem on a donkey.
• Jesus turns his last Passover supper into a memorial.
• Jesus prays in agony in the Garden of Gethsemane.
• He is arrested and tried by Annas, Caiaphas, and Pontius Pilate.

### DEATH AND RESURRECTION

*Jesus dies on the cross*

• Jesus is crucified by the Romans.
• Jesus' mother and other female disciples stand by the cross as he dies.
• The Roman centurion says, "Surely this man was the Son of God!"
• On the third day, the women find Jesus' tomb empty.
• He appears alive to his disciples, and they finally believe in Jesus' resurrection from the dead.

*Herod waits for Jesus to be brought for trial*

## THE RULE OF THE HERODS

During New Testament times, the Romans appointed local kings, known as Herods. When the first Herod was appointed in Palestine, some Jews were ready to think he was the king promised by the prophets, even though he was not descended from David. Most Jews hated Herod's rule and "king of the Jews" was a title given to him by the Romans. Herod died soon after Jesus' birth. Years later, when Jesus was accused of blasphemy, he was brought for trial before Herod's son Antipas. In doubt, Herod passed Jesus on to Pontius Pilate.

HEROD ANTIPAS
*This painting of Herod is by Duccio di Buoninsegna (c.1278–1318).*

EASTER, PALM SUNDAY
Throughout the world, Palm Sunday, just before Easter, marks the day when Jesus rode into Jerusalem on a donkey and the crowds shouted "Hosanna!" and threw palm leaves onto the road in front of him. Then follows the sorrow of Good Friday, and the joy of Easter Day when Jesus' resurrection is celebrated.

## THE GOSPEL WRITERS

The Gospels, from a Greek word meaning "good news," were written over a period of about fifty years. Two of the writers, Matthew and John, were members of Jesus' twelve disciples, while Mark was a young follower who lived in Jerusalem. Luke was a Gentile who possibly never met Jesus. The first three Gospel writers highlight different aspects of Jesus' life, while John reflects on the meaning of his life and death.

THE FOUR EVANGELISTS, OR GOSPEL WRITERS
*This stone carving from Mt. St. Michel in France depicts (from left to right) Mark, John, Luke, and Matthew.*

## PAUL'S JOURNEYS

The apostle Paul was the chief missionary of the early church. He was called by God to spread the message of Jesus as far as possible, to both Jews and Gentiles. He undertook many long and dangerous journeys, and finally went to stand trial in Rome, the center of the empire. "The love of Christ urges me on," he said, "for he died for all!"

ROUTE MAP
*This map shows the route Paul took on his third main journey. He had visited many of these places before.*

### PAUL'S EPISTLES

Paul wrote letters to keep in touch with the churches he founded. In the New Testament they appear in order of length, starting with the longest.

| Paul's Letters | Date AD | Written in |
| --- | --- | --- |
| Romans | 57 | Corinth |
| 1 Corinthians | 55 | Ephesus |
| 2 Corinthians | 55 | Macedonia |
| Galatians | 49 | Antioch |
| Ephesians | 60 | Rome |
| Philippians | 61 | Rome |
| Colossians | 60 | Rome |
| 1 Thessalonians | 51 | Corinth |
| 2 Thessalonians | 51 | Corinth |
| 1 Timothy | 63–65 | Philippi |
| 2 Timothy | 63–65 | Rome |
| Titus | 63–65 | Rome |
| Philemon | 60 | Rome |

# JOHN AND JESUS

THE MIRACULOUS births of Jesus and his cousin John occurred within the same year in the province of Judea, Palestine. With them, the story of Christianity began. John was chosen by God to prepare people for the arrival of Jesus, the Messiah. During his ministry, Jesus inspired people to believe in the Kingdom of God.

*John the Baptist spreads the word*

## JOHN THE BAPTIST

Meaning: *God is merciful*
Appears: *Matt. 3, 4, 11, 14, 21; Mark 1, 6; Luke 1, 3, 7, 9; John 1, 3, 10*

The longed-for son of Elizabeth and Zechariah, John was a prophet who, dressed in clothes made of camel's hair, preached in the Judean desert. He told the crowds who flocked to hear him that a greater person than himself was soon to appear, and that they should prepare for this by repenting of their sins. John became known as "the Baptist" because he baptized people in the Jordan River, an act that represented the washing away of sins. After leaving Judea, John was put in prison and later beheaded by Herod Antipas because John criticized him for marrying his sister-in-law, Herodias.

## ELIZABETH

Meaning: *God is an oath*
Appears: *Luke 1*

Elizabeth, cousin of Mary, and her husband Zechariah, prayed for a child for many years. God answered their plea and gave them the son who was to become John the Baptist.

*Zechariah writes "His name is John"*

*Elizabeth holds the baby boy in her arms*

## GABRIEL

Meaning: *God is mighty*
Appears: *Luke 1; Daniel 8, 9*

Gabriel was an angel of the highest order, also known as an archangel. He is one of three angels who are mentioned by name in the Bible; the others are Michael and Raphael. It was Gabriel who brought God's words to Daniel, an Old Testament prophet, and also to Zechariah and to Mary. He foretold the births of John the Baptist and Jesus.

*Gabriel brings good news to Zechariah*

## ZECHARIAH

Meaning: *God has remembered*
Appears: *Luke 1*

Father of John the Baptist, Zechariah was also a priest. One day, while Zechariah was offering incense at the temple, the archangel Gabriel appeared to him and announced that he and his wife Elizabeth, who was barren, were to have a son. The boy would be called John and would prepare Israel for the Messiah. At first, Zechariah did not believe the angel's words, so his power of speech was taken away until his baby had been named. Zechariah then sang the *Benedictus*, praising God for his gift.

## SALOME

Meaning: *Peace*
Appears: *Matt. 14; Mark 6*

Daughter of Herodias and her first husband Philip, Salome danced before her stepfather, Herod Antipas. Prompted by her mother, she then asked for John the Baptist's head as a reward. Although Salome's actual name is not used in the Bible, it was recorded by the Jewish historian Josephus.

## HERODIAS

Meaning: *unknown*
Appears: *Matt. 14; Mark 6*

Mother of Salome and second wife of Herod Antipas, scheming Herodias resented John the Baptist for publicly condemning her marriage to Herod. She was indirectly responsible for John's beheading.

HERODIAS

*Jesus turns water into wine – his first miracle*

before his death, Jesus chose twelve disciples who he could trust to help with his ministry and carry on his work. Opposition to Jesus grew among the authorities, and he was eventually crucified. On the third day, he rose from the dead. Today, Christianity is one of the world's main religions with about 1.75 billion believers who follow Jesus' teaching.

## MARY

Meaning: *Unknown*

Appears: *Matt. 1, 2; Luke 1, 2; John 19*

Mary was probably only a teenager when she received the news – known as the Annunciation – from the angel Gabriel that she would be the mother of the son of God. Mary traveled with Joseph from her home in Nazareth to Bethlehem, where she gave birth to Jesus.

## JESUS

Meaning: *God saves*

Appears: *Throughout the Gospels*

Jesus is the son of God who was sent to establish God's Kingdom on earth. During his ministry he performed miracles, including healing the sick, which brought people from far and wide seeking his help. Crowds were captivated by his teaching. Jesus used simple stories about everyday life, known as parables, to convey his message. He said that the Kingdom of God was coming and challenged people to give up everything and follow him. Some thought he was going to start a violent revolution against the Romans, but instead he taught his followers to love their enemies. In line with this teaching, he reached out to help those on the fringes of society, such as prostitutes and lawbreakers, which offended some people. About three years

*Joseph and Mary could find nowhere to stay*

## JOHN BAPTIZES JESUS

Jesus went to the Jordan River to be baptized by John. Although Jesus had no need to repent of any sin, he wanted to be baptized so that he could set an example to others. This event marked the beginning of Jesus' ministry.

*John gently lowers Jesus into the water*

**The act of baptism**

Ritual cleansing was a daily duty for Jews. When John baptized people, he was obeying Jewish law as well as making the act of washing a symbol of forgiveness and a new start. After Jesus' baptism, the voice of God was heard saying "This is my beloved son, in whom I am well pleased."

**Ritual purification**

These excavations at Qumran, in modern-day Israel, reveal a bath that was once used for purification, or cleansing. The ritual involved total immersion.

## JOSEPH

Meaning: *God adds*

Appears: *Matt. 1, 2; Luke 2; John 6*

Joseph was the husband of Mary, the mother of Jesus. Like Mary, he lived in Nazareth, in Galilee. Before Joseph married Mary, he discovered that she was pregnant, but an angel assured him that the child was from God. Soon after the birth, the angel warned Joseph of Herod the Great's plan to kill Jesus, and so Joseph took his family to safety in Egypt. After Herod's death, they returned to Nazareth, where Joseph taught Jesus his trade as a carpenter. Joseph was a descendant of David which fulfilled the prophecy that the Messiah would be the "Son of David."

### SEE ALSO

✝ Daniel p 34

✝ Herod the Great pp 48–49

✝ Herod Antipas p 48

# PEOPLE OF THE GOSPELS

THE GOSPELS RECORD the life and teachings of Jesus and introduce many of the people of his time. Jesus began his ministry in the small province of Galilee, where he was raised. He then traveled throughout Samaria and Judea, preaching to people from all walks of life. Unlike the other rabbis, Jesus included women, such as Mary Magdalene, Joanna, and Susanna, among his followers.

*Simeon rejoices at the Savior's birth*

*Anna admires the baby Jesus*

## JAMES

Meaning: *He grasps, holds tight*
Appears: *Matt. 13; Mark 6; Acts 12, 15, 21; 1 Cor. 15; Gal. 1, 2; James 1; Jude 1*
According to the Gospels of Matthew and Mark, James was one of Jesus' four brothers. At first, Jesus' brothers did not believe that Jesus was the Messiah. When James witnessed the Resurrection of Jesus, he became a believer and later led the church in Jerusalem. He wrote the letter of James in the Bible.

JAMES

## JUDE

Meaning: *Praised*
Appears: *Matt. 13; Mark 6; Jude 1*
Jude, also known as Judas, is believed to be the author of the New Testament letter of Jude. In the letter, he describes himself as "a servant of Jesus Christ, and brother of James." The Gospels of both Matthew and Mark mention that Jude was also a brother of Jesus, along with James, Joseph, and Simon. He became a respected leader and teacher, working to keep the Church true to Jesus' message.

## SIMEON

Meaning: *God hears*
Appears: *Luke 2*
A devout man, Simeon was told by God that he would see the Messiah before he died. He was visiting the temple in Jerusalem when Mary and Joseph took Jesus there to be blessed. Simeon approached them, took the baby in his arms, and announced he was the long-awaited Savior. Simeon's words of praise, the *Nunc Dimittis*, are still sung in church today.

## ANNA

Meaning: *God is gracious*
Appears: *Luke 2*
An 84 year-old widow, who was also a prophetess, Anna spent all her time in the temple, fasting and praying. She joined Simeon in thanking God for letting them see Jesus. Anna then helped spread the good news about the Savior throughout Jerusalem.

## SIMON THE PHARISEE

Meaning: *God hears*
Appears: *Luke 7*
Simon belonged to the Pharisees, a group whose members believed in strict observation of the Jewish religious laws. He invited Jesus to eat with him, and during the meal, a prostitute came into the room, crying. She bathed Jesus' feet with her tears and anointed them with perfume. Simon was shocked by this and decided that Jesus must also be a sinner. Jesus then challenged Simon's reaction, explaining that the woman needed their love and forgiveness.

*Simon criticizes Jesus for touching a sinner*

## MARY MAGDALENE

Meaning: *Mary from Magdala*
Appears: *Matt. 27, 28; Mark 15, 16; Luke 8, 24; John 19, 20*
A devoted follower of Jesus, Mary had been cured by him of evil spirits and disease. She traveled with Jesus during his ministry and stood beside him while he died on the cross. Mary was one of the first to meet Jesus after he rose from the dead. John's Gospel tells that, after finding the tomb empty, Mary saw Jesus but did not recognize him until he gently spoke her name.

MARY MAGDALENE
*Detail from a painting by Georges de la Tour (1593–1662)*

## JOANNA

Meaning: *God is gracious*
Appears: *Luke 8, 24*

Another female disciple, Joanna was married to a wealthy official, Chuza. She was able to offer money to help Jesus and the apostles. With Mary Magdalene, she brought news of Jesus' resurrection to the other disciples.

## SUSANNA

Meaning: *Lily, lotus flower*
Appears: *Luke 8*

Susanna also appears in the list of women disciples. It was unheard of at the time for a rabbi to have female disciples. It was even more amazing that Jesus traveled with them and let them provide money. Some rabbis believed that women could not learn God's law.

## JAIRUS

Meaning: *God enlightens*
Appears: *Mark 5; Luke 8*

Jairus was a ruler of the synagogue in Capernaum, where he organized and led the services.

*Jairus and his wife greet their daughter*

When his twelve-year-old daughter fell ill, Jairus asked Jesus to his home, hoping that he would heal her. On the way, one of Jairus's servants brought news that the girl was dead. Jesus continued to the house and told the people who had gathered around him to wait outside, saying the girl was not dead but sleeping. He brought Jairus's daughter back to life, but told the three disciples with him to keep what he had done a secret.

## BARTIMAEUS

Meaning: *Son of Timaeus*
Appears: *Mark 10; Luke 18*

Bartimaeus was a blind man who begged beside the road near Jericho. When Jesus and his disciples passed by, Bartimaeus started shouting, not for money but to be healed. Jesus stopped and asked what he wanted. "Rabbi, I want to see," he replied. Bartimaeus's faith was rewarded, and Jesus restored his sight.

## NICODEMUS

Meaning: *Conqueror of the people*
Appears: *John 3, 7, 19*

A chief Pharisee in Jerusalem, Nicodemus was fascinated by Jesus' work and went to see him. When Jesus told him, "You must be born again" – meaning he must undergo a spiritual rebirth – Nicodemus was puzzled and did not know how to respond. Later, Jesus stopped to speak to a poor woman by a well in Samaria.

*Nicodemus goes to see Jesus at night*

*Jesus tells him that he must be "born again"*

## THE GOSPEL WRITERS

The four accounts of Jesus' life and teachings were written over approximately fifty years and each one portrays him in a different light. Mark presents Jesus as a healer; Matthew focuses more on Jesus' teaching; Luke shows him as the Savior of the world; and John presents him as the giver of eternal life. Two of the Gospel authors are traditionally believed to have been Jesus' apostles – Matthew, the former tax collector from Capernaum, and John, who was the apostle "whom Jesus loved."

She was neither wealthy nor educated like Nicodemus, but when Jesus challenged her, she and the people of her village responded gladly. John, who tells the story in his Gospel, contrasts Nicodemus's doubt with the Samaritan woman's faith. However, when Jesus was later condemned by the religious leaders, Nicodemus did ask that he should have a fair hearing.

MATTHEW    MARK    LUKE    JOHN

THE FOUR AUTHORS
*This 15th-century stained-glass window from Bourges Cathedral, France, depicts the four Gospel writers.*

### SEE ALSO

✝ Jesus p 41
✝ John p 46
✝ Matthew p 47
✝ Mark p 52
✝ Luke p 53

## MARY OF BETHANY

Meaning: *Mary from Bethany*
Appears: *Matt. 26; Mark 14;*
*Luke 10; John 11, 12*
Sister of Martha and Lazarus, Mary was a close friend of Jesus, who often visited them at their home in Bethany. According to John's Gospel, it was Mary who anointed Jesus with expensive perfume and wiped his feet with her hair. Judas Iscariot was shocked by this extravagance but was rebuked by Jesus.

**Martha** knows that Jesus has the power to heal

## MARTHA

Meaning: *Lady, mistress*
Appears: *Luke 10; John 11, 12*
Martha was the sister of Mary and Lazarus. She was more practical than her sister, and took charge of running the household. Martha once complained to Jesus that Mary spent too much time listening to his teachings, instead of doing her chores. However, Jesus supported Mary by saying that she had chosen to spend her time wisely.

**Mary** nurses her brother Lazarus, who is taken ill

BURIAL GROUNDS
*Lazarus's tomb would have looked similar to this one in Israel.*

## LAZARUS

Meaning: *God has helped*
Appears: *John 11, 12*
The brother of Mary and Martha, Lazarus was brought back to life by Jesus after dying from a sudden illness. Crowds watched as Lazarus, still wrapped in his shroud, emerged from his tomb four days after he had died. As a result of this miracle, many people began to believe in the words of Jesus.

**Lazarus** lies close to death

## ZACCHAEUS

Meaning: *God remembers*
Appears: *Luke 19*
Zacchaeus was a rich tax collector, who had amassed his wealth through dishonest means. When he heard that Jesus was passing by, he climbed a tree to get a better view of the teacher. Zacchaeus was amazed when Jesus stopped under the tree and invited himself to Zacchaeus's house (tax collectors were usually shunned by Jewish society). Zacchaeus repented by giving half his possessions to the poor and paying back four times the amount he had stolen.

**Zacchaeus** welcomes Jesus to his home

## THE GOOD SAMARITAN

Jesus often taught using parables – tales of daily life with a hidden message. The story of the Good Samaritan (Luke 10:25–37) tells of a man who has been viciously attacked. A priest and a Levite both ignore him and cross to the other side of the road. A Samaritan stops and gently tends the wounds of the injured man. The parable illustrates Jesus' message to "love your neighbor as yourself."

A TRUE NEIGHBOR
*This image, by Joseph Heinemann (1825–1901), shows the Samaritan and the Jew, who were usually sworn enemies.*

## SIMON THE LEPER

Meaning: *God hears*
Appears: *Matt. 26; Mark 14*
A friend of Jesus, Simon the Leper lived in Bethany. The term "leper" was used to describe anyone with a skin disease. Simon had probably been cured of his illness, since lepers were considered impure and had to live away from the towns in isolation. It was during a meal in Simon's house, just before Jesus died, that Mary of Bethany showed her love for Jesus by anointing him.

*Roman soldier on the road to Calvary*

*Simon of Cyrene is forced to take Jesus' cross*

JOSEPH OF ARIMATHEA

## MALCHUS

Meaning: *King*
Appears: *Matt.26; Mark 14; Luke 22; John 18*
A servant of Caiaphas, the high priest, Malchus went to the Garden of Gethsemane with the soldiers who arrested Jesus there. The disciple Peter tried to stop them. He drew his sword and attacked Malchus, cutting off his right ear. But, according to Luke's Gospel, Jesus said "No more of this!" then healed Malchus's ear.

## BARABBAS

Meaning: *Son of Abba*
Appears: *Matt. 27; Mark 15; Luke 23; John 18*
A Jewish freedom-fighter, Barabbas had been arrested by the Romans and was awaiting execution at the time of Jesus' trial. The Roman governor, Pontius Pilate, usually released one Jewish prisoner at Passover. He allowed the crowds to decide between Barabbas and Jesus. They chose Barabbas, so Jesus the innocent died instead of Barabbas the murderer.

*BARABBAS IN CHAINS*

## SIMON OF CYRENE

Meaning: *God hears*
Appears: *Matt. 27; Mark 15; Luke 23*
A Jew from Cyrene, in North Africa, Simon was visiting Jerusalem for Passover at the time of Jesus' death. The Roman soldiers picked Simon out of the crowd and made him carry Jesus' cross for him.

## MARY

Meaning: *unknown*
Appears: *Matt. 27, 28; Mark 15; Luke 24*
Mary was the mother of James the younger and Joses. She stood beside the cross while Jesus died.

## SALOME

Meaning: *Peace*
Appears: *Mark 15, 16*
Mother of the disciples James and John, Salome was one of the women at the foot of the cross during Jesus' crucifixion. According to Mark, she went with Mary Magdalene to anoint Jesus' body and found the tomb empty. An angel told them that Jesus had risen from the dead.

## JOSEPH OF ARIMATHEA

Meaning: *God adds*
Appears: *Matt. 27; Mark 15; Luke 23; John 19*
A wealthy and influential Jew and member of the ruling council, Joseph became a secret disciple of Jesus. When Jesus died, he asked Pilate for the body, which he reverently

*Cleopas and a fellow traveler persuade Jesus to share a meal with them*

*Jesus breaks bread and gives thanks before disappearing*

wrapped in a clean linen cloth. Then he and Nicodemus buried Jesus in a new, unoccupied tomb cut out of the rock, and rolled a large boulder across the entrance.

## CLEOPAS

Meaning: *Father of glory, fame*
Appears: *Luke 24; John 19*
Cleopas was one of Jesus' disciples. He and a friend unknowingly met the risen Christ while walking on the road from Jerusalem to Emmaus. They invited this man to eat with them. Only after hearing him speak, and seeing him break and share the bread, did they realize it was Jesus.

SEE ALSO
✝ Caiaphas p 49
✝ Pontius Pilate p 50

# THE TWELVE DISCIPLES

JESUS' REPUTATION GREW, and he soon attracted a large group of disciples who spent as much time as they could listening to him and helping him in his ministry. As time went by, Jesus decided to appoint a small group of disciples he could trust. He spent a whole night in prayer before choosing twelve men who could lead the church after his death and resurrection. Jesus called them apostles, which means "sent ones," because he sent them out to continue his work.

*ANDREW*

## ANDREW

Meaning: *Brave*
Appears: *Matt. 4, 10; Mark 1, 3, 13; Luke 6; John 1, 6, 12; Acts 1*
Andrew was Simon Peter's brother, and the first to meet Jesus. He immediately thought Jesus could be the Messiah and introduced his brother. It was Andrew who found the boy with loaves and fish for Jesus' miraculous feeding of the five thousand.

## JAMES

Meaning: *He grasps, holds tight*
Appears: *Matt. 4, 10, 17; Mark 1, 3, 5, 9, 10, 13,14; Luke 5, 6, 8, 9; Acts 1, 12*
James was the son of Zebedee and brother of John, who was also one of the Twelve. James, with John, Peter, and Andrew, were all fishermen on Lake Galilee when Jesus called them to be disciples. Later, James, Peter, and John became especially close to Jesus and were with him at some very significant events. These included the Transfiguration (see illustration), when Jesus appeared to them as a heavenly being. James was killed by Herod Agrippa I.

## JOHN

Meaning: *God is gracious*
Appears: *In the Gospels; Acts 1, 3, 4, 8, 12*
John was the son of Zebedee and the brother of James. Jesus called them the "sons of thunder," because of their fiery tempers. John wanted to call down fire from heaven on Jesus' enemies, the Samaritans. He also stopped a man who was not a disciple from performing exorcisms in Jesus' name. Jesus tamed their wildness and John went on to be a popular teacher, possibly the author of John's Gospel.

*Peter denies knowing Jesus*

*A servant girl says she saw Peter with Jesus*

## SIMON PETER

Meaning: *God hears (Simon); The rock (Peter)*
Appears: *Throughout the New Testament, especially Luke 5; Matt. 14, 16, 26; John 21; Acts 10*
A fisherman in Galilee, Peter became the leader of the twelve disciples. Simon was the Jewish name he was given as a child, but Peter was the name Jesus chose when he called him to be an apostle. He said, "You are Peter, and on this Rock I will build my church." Despite his deep faith, Peter was not always a loyal disciple. He told Jesus he would never deny him, but when Jesus was arrested Peter's nerve failed, and three times he denied knowing him. After the Resurrection, Jesus met with Peter to restore his love. Peter went on to become head of the early church and Roman Catholic Christians regard him as the first Pope.

*Jesus*

*Moses*

*Elijah*

*James sees Jesus in a bright cloud*

*John hears the voice of God*

*Peter*

## PHILIP

Meaning: *Lover of horses*
Appears: *John 1, 6; Acts 1*
Philip was a friend of Peter and Andrew, from the town of Bethsaida. He believed immediately that Jesus was the Messiah but faced some testing questions from Jesus that stretched his faith.

## BARTHOLOMEW

Meaning: *Son of Ptolemy*
Appears: *In the Gospels; Acts 1*
Bartholomew may be the same person as Nathanael, mentioned in John's Gospel. If so, he was a passionate Israelite who accepted that Jesus was "the Son of God, the King of Israel."

## THOMAS

Meaning: *Twin*
Appears: *John 20*
Referred to as "the twin" in John's Gospel, Thomas was not with the others when they first saw Jesus risen from the dead. He refused to believe their story unless he could touch Jesus' wounds. A week later, Jesus appeared to him so he would stop doubting and believe.

## MATTHEW

Meaning: *Gift of God*
Appears: *Matt. 9, 10; Mark 3; Luke 6; Acts 1*
Matthew may also have been called Levi. He worked for King Herod and many people thought he was a traitor. He was so attracted by Jesus' ideas that he left his post and followed him. He gave a party to introduce Jesus to his friends.

*Jesus has nail marks on his body*

*Doubting Thomas feels Jesus' wounds*

*Matthew was a tax collector for Herod Antipas*

## JAMES

Meaning: *Holds tight*
Appears: *Matt. 10; Mark 3; Luke 6; Acts 1*
Little is known about this disciple, except that he was the son of Alphaeus. This was also the name of Levi's father, so James may have been Matthew's brother.

## THADDAEUS

Meaning: *Loving, compassionate*
Appears: *Matt. 10; Mark 3*
Thaddaeus is also called "Judas, son of James" in two lists of the Twelve Apostles. Perhaps he preferred the name Thaddaeus after Judas Iscariot betrayed Jesus.

## SIMON THE ZEALOT

Meaning: *God hears*
Appears: *Matt. 10; Mark 3; Luke 6; Acts 1*
Simon may have belonged to the Zealots – a group of freedom-fighters who challenged Roman forces occupying the land. When he became a disciple, Simon lived alongside Matthew the tax collector, a person he previously would have hated as a traitor.

## JUDAS ISCARIOT

Meaning: *Praised*
Appears: *In the Gospels; Acts 1*
Although he was a disciple, Judas betrayed Jesus to the Jewish authorities by leading soldiers to the Garden of Gethsamene, then identifying him with a kiss. The Gospels say he did it for thirty silver coins. Judas was so sorry afterward that he gave the money back and hanged himself.

*Judas looked after the disciples' money*

## THE LAST SUPPER

Just before he died, Jesus gathered his disciples for a last Passover celebration. During the meal, Jesus revealed that one of them would betray him. They all became uncomfortable not knowing who it was. Eventually Jesus whispered to John that it was Judas. This last meal is celebrated today as Mass or Holy Communion.

Thaddeus  James  Matthew  Simon  John  Jesus  Peter  James  Judas  Bartholomew  Philip  Andrew  Thomas

### SEE ALSO

✝ Herod Antipas p 48
✝ Herod Agrippa I p 48
✝ Zebedee p 61

# LEADERS IN PALESTINE

**Herod Antipas** *watches Salome*

THE ROMANS WERE the overall rulers in Palestine during the era of the New Testament. They tried to ensure the loyalty of local leaders by installing local kings – the Herods – on their thrones. The Romans also appointed high priests, who were not only religious leaders for the Jews but also wielded considerable political power. Because of their connection with the Romans, the Herods were very unpopular with their Jewish subjects. This led to several revolts – each one savagely suppressed by the Romans.

## HEROD THE GREAT

Meaning: *unknown*
Appears: *Matt. 2; Luke 1*
This is the Herod who founded the dynasty, or line, of Herods who ruled in Palestine from 37 BC onward. He became friendly with the Roman Emperor Augustus, who gave Herod the title "King of the Jews" – when Palestine already had a Jewish king. A bitter civil war broke out, which lasted until Herod, helped by the Romans, took over the throne. He then ruled until just after Jesus was born in 4 BC. Toward the end of his reign, Herod imagined that everyone was plotting against him. He even had three of his sons and his wife, Mariamne, murdered. When the wise men arrived with news of the birth of Jesus, the King of the Jews, he ordered the massacre of the innocents – that all baby boys in Bethlehem must be killed.

**Herod** *listens closely to reports of a new king*

*Three wise men arrive from the east*

## HEROD ARCHELAUS

Meaning: *Ruler of the people*
Appears: *Matt. 2*
When Herod the Great died, his kingdom was divided among his three sons, and Archelaus inherited the southern part, Judea. He was a terrible ruler who was deposed by the Romans after ten years.

*HEROD ARCHELAUS*

## HEROD PHILIP

Meaning: *Lover of horses*
Appears: *Luke 3*
Herod the Great had two sons named Philip. The first did not become a ruler but lost his wife Herodias to his half-brother Antipas. The second, Herod Philip, ruled the northeastern part of Palestine. Unlike his brothers, he was just and good, and reigned until his death in AD 33.

## HEROD ANTIPAS

Meaning: *possibly Opponent*
Appears: *Matt. 14; Mark 6, 8; Luke 3, 9, 13, 23*
Antipas inherited Galilee from his father Herod the Great, and ruled there until he was deposed by the Romans in AD 39. It was Herod Antipas who gave John the Baptist's head to his stepdaughter Salome. He was intrigued when he heard about Jesus and wanted to see him perform a miracle, but Jesus called him "that fox" and refused to visit. Eventually Jesus appeared before Herod at his trial, but refused to answer Herod's questions.

## HEROD AGRIPPA I

Meaning: *Catcher of horses*
Appears: *Acts 12*
Agrippa was the grandson of Herod the Great, and the brother of Herodias. The Romans made him ruler of his grandfather's kingdom after Antipas and Philip. He was very popular with the Jews and tried to win greater popularity by killing the apostle James and imprisoning Peter. But Peter was miraculously released from prison by an angel the night before his execution. Agrippa died dramatically in AD 44 – he was eaten alive by worms. In fact, it was probably intestinal disease.

## HEROD AGRIPPA II

Meaning: *Catcher of horses*

Appears: Acts 25, 26

Son of Herod Agrippa I, this Herod was only seventeen when his father died but was given the kingdom later by the Emperor Claudius. He was ruler during the Jewish rising against Rome that began in AD 66. He also had a famous encounter with the apostle Paul, who made a speech describing how he had become a Christian on the road to Damascus. Agrippa teasingly replied, "You're trying to make me a Christian on the spot!"

***Caiaphas*** *accuses Jesus of blasphemy*

## BERNICE

Meaning: *Victorious*

Appears: Acts 25

Bernice was the eldest daughter of Herod Agrippa I. She was with her brother, Agrippa II, when he had his encounter with the apostle Paul. At that point she had already married and deserted several husbands. She later became mistress of Emperor Titus. Bernice and her sister Drusilla were both regarded as shameless women.

## ANNAS

Meaning: *God is gracious*

Appears: Luke 3; John 18; Acts 4

Annas was made high priest of the Jews in AD 6, but was officially deposed by the Romans in AD 15. However, he continued to exercise great power because the Jews believed that high priests were appointed for life. Luke still called him "high priest," and Annas went on to chair one of the tribunals that questioned Jesus before his crucifixion.

## CAIAPHAS

Meaning: *possibly Valleys*

Appears: Matt. 26; Luke 3; John 11, 18; Acts 4

High priest from AD 18–36, Caiaphas was a much respected leader of the Jews. He was the son-in-law of Annas and shared his power and prestige. Caiaphas presided over Jesus' trial. When Jesus claimed to be the son of God, Caiaphas accused him of blasphemy. He later tried to prevent the first Christians from preaching about Jesus – without success.

## ANANIAS

Meaning: *God is gracious*

Appears: Acts 23, 24

Known for his greed, Ananias was high priest from AD 47–58. He chaired the ruling Jewish Council when the apostle Paul appeared before them, and behaved cruelly toward Paul by asking bystanders to strike him on the mouth. He was murdered in AD 66 for sympathizing with Rome.

## HEROD THE GREAT

Herod and his sons were all passionate builders. They created palaces for themselves, temples for various gods, and founded new towns, such as Tiberias and Caesarea, named after Roman emperors.

### Herod's Temple

Herod's most famous project was rebuilding the temple in Jerusalem. Started in 19 BC, the building was still underway almost fifty years later, when Jesus overturned the tables of the money-changers there (see John 2:13–22). Sadly, it was destroyed by the Romans in AD 70.

*MODEL OF HEROD'S TEMPLE*

**Divided kingdom**

This map shows the way Herod the Great's kingdom was divided after his death among his three sons, Archelaus, Antipas, and Philip. At the time of Jesus, Judea was ruled by the Romans. The area became a united kingdom again under Herod Agrippa I.

## GAMALIEL

Meaning: *Reward of God*

Appears: Acts 5, 22

According to Luke's Gospel, Gamaliel was a famous teacher of Jewish law who was "held in honor by all the people." When the Jewish authorities arrested the apostles for preaching about Jesus, Gamaliel advised them to release the apostles. He reasoned that if God was behind the new Christian movement, "you cannot overthrow it." If false, then it would soon fade away. One of Gamaliel's most famous pupils was young Saul, who became the apostle Paul. Saul's parents sent him to Jerusalem so that he could learn from Gamaliel.

*Member of the Jewish Council*

***Gamaliel*** *suggests freeing the apostles*

### SEE ALSO

✦ John the Baptist p 40

✦ Peter p 46

✦ Paul p 52

# ROMAN RULERS

By THE TIME OF Jesus' ministry, Palestine had been under Roman rule for one hundred years. People were used to the presence of Roman soldiers, especially in the towns, but they never got used to paying taxes to Rome. The Jews believed that they were God's people and did not like being ruled by a pagan power. Some Jews – including one of Jesus' disciples, Simon the Zealot – became members of armed resistance groups, and tension in the region ran high.

*A BUST OF EMPEROR AUGUSTUS*

## AUGUSTUS

Meaning: *The revered one*
Appears: *Luke 2*
Augustus, originally named Octavian, was the first emperor of Rome. He brought stability to the empire after a period of great turmoil, and reigned from 27 BC–AD 14. Augustus was emperor when Jesus was born. He called the census that forced Joseph and Mary to travel to Bethlehem just before the birth of Jesus. The purpose of the census, which Augustus started to hold in some parts of the empire every seven years, was to see how many people should be paying taxes. This caused a great deal of resentment and meant that Jesus was born into a troubled society.

## TIBERIUS

Meaning: *Named after the god Tiber*
Appears: *Luke 3*
Tiberius was Augustus's nephew by marriage. With no surviving children of his own, Augustus chose Tiberius as his heir. Tiberius was emperor from AD 14–37, through the years of Jesus' life and crucifixion. He was not a popular emperor.

*EMPEROR TIBERIUS*

## CLAUDIUS

Meaning: *possibly Lame*
Appears: *Acts 11, 18*
Roman emperor from AD 41–54, Claudius was initially tolerant of Jewish religious practices. However, in AD 49 he issued a decree commanding all the Jews in Rome to leave the city because of rioting in the Jewish community there. Two of the banished Jews – Priscilla and Aquila – traveled to Corinth, where they met Paul and became his close friends. After Claudius's death, the Jews gradually returned to Rome. Records show that Claudius suffered from paralysis, which may explain his name.

## QUIRINIUS

Meaning: *Warlike*
Appears: *Luke 2*
Luke's gospel tells us that Quirinius was the Roman governor of Syria, and was responsible for overseeing the census at the time of Jesus' birth. Unfortunately, the dates are hard to confirm. From Roman sources we learn that Quirinius was governor of Syria from AD 6–9, and that he held a census then. But Jesus was born ten years earlier. Biblical scholars are still puzzled about this but think that riots when Herod Archelaus was removed may have confused Luke's dates.

## PONTIUS PILATE

Meaning: *Armed with a spear*
Appears: *Matt. 27; Mark 15; Luke 3, 13, 23; John 18, 19; Acts 3, 4, 13; 1 Tim. 6*
The name of Pontius Pilate is forever linked with the death of Jesus. Roman

***Pontius Pilate** washes his hands of Jesus' death*

governor of Judea from AD 26–36, Pilate was known for his cruelty to the Jews. When Jesus came before Pilate for trial, Pilate wanted to release him because he knew he was innocent. But when Jesus' enemies insisted he should be put to death, Pilate washed his hands in public to absolve himself of Jesus' murder before ordering his crucifixion.

## SERGIUS PAULUS

Meaning: *Little (Paulus)*
Appears: *Acts 13*
According to Luke, Sergius Paulus was an intelligent man. He was the Roman proconsul, or governor, of Cyprus where Paul and Barnabas caused a stir by preaching the Gospel. Sergius summoned them to appear before him because he wanted to hear more. Sergius eventually became a Christian.

*SERGIUS PAULUS*

## GALLIO

Meaning: *unknown*
Appears: *Acts 18*
Gallio was the Roman proconsul of Achaia in Greece from AD 52–53, at the time when Paul was in Corinth. Paul's Jewish opponents tried to accuse him, but Gallio refused to listen because the charges were religious, not criminal. Gallio killed himself after a failed plot to murder Nero.

*GALLIO*

## CLAUDIUS LYSIAS

Meaning: *unknown*
Appears: *Acts 23, 24*
Claudius Lysias was the commander of the Roman garrison in Jerusalem. He rescued Paul from the middle of a riot in the temple. Later, tipped off by Paul's nephew, he sent Paul under armed guard to Caesarea to keep him safe.

## FELIX

Meaning: *Happy*
Appears: *Acts 23, 24*
Noted for his greed, Felix was governor of Judea from AD 52–59. When Paul was a prisoner in Caesarea, Felix kept him locked up without trial, hoping Paul would pay a bribe for his release. When Paul spoke to him about God's judgment of evil, Felix became frightened.

## DRUSILLA

Meaning: *unknown*
Appears: *Acts 24*
Drusilla was the wife of Felix, and the younger sister of Bernice and Herod Agrippa II. While she was still a teenager, Felix enticed her away from her first husband to be Felix's third wife. Drusilla was anxious to hear Paul talk about his faith in Jesus.

## FESTUS

Meaning: *Sacred*
Appears: *Acts 24, 25, 26*
When Festus became governor of Judea after Felix, he inherited Paul as his prisoner. He tried to resolve Paul's case, but Paul wanted to be tried in Rome to avoid being killed by his enemies. Paul made a powerful defense speech in front of Festus, who accused him of being mad.

## LIFE IN TIBERIUS'S EMPIRE

The Roman Empire was vast and, at the time of the New Testament, included most of the countries around the Mediterranean Sea. The Romans introduced their style of building and their system of government into the conquered areas.

*A ROMAN POETRY READING*

**Roman way of life**
Romans had a high standard of living wherever they were posted. Women, such as Drusilla, could enjoy a great deal of independence and often had a lot of influence. This scene is painted by Sir Lawrence Alma-Tadema.

**Soldiers**
People in Palestine often saw Roman soldiers on the street. Usually they would not carry their legionary standard because Jews believed it was an offense to display images. On one occasion, Pontius Pilate ordered his troops to enter Jerusalem displaying the standards. A demonstration by the Jews forced him to remove them.

*ROMAN SOLDIERS WITH STANDARD*

*Festus agrees to let Paul face trial in Rome*

## JULIUS

Meaning: *unknown*
Appears: *Acts 27*
Julius was the kind Roman centurion who allowed Paul off the ship to visit friends during the journey to Rome. He was helped by Paul when they were shipwrecked.

## PUBLIUS

Meaning: *unknown*
Appears: *Acts 28*
Publius was the leading citizen of Malta when Paul was shipwrecked. He invited Paul to stay at his home. While there, Paul healed Publius's father of dystentery.

### SEE ALSO

✝ Paul p 52
✝ Barnabas p 52
✝ Priscilla and Aquila p 56

# THE FIRST MISSIONARIES

THE STORY OF THE first Christians centers on those whose mission it was to pass on the good news about Jesus. Most Christians did this in a small way, but some devoted all their time to spreading the message. It was not long before the news had been taken around the Mediterranean world, and beyond.

*Paul writes letters while under house arrest in Rome*

A soldier guards the door

## PAUL

Meaning: *Small*

Appears: *196 verses in the New Testament, esp. Acts 7– 9, 13*

When he is first mentioned, Paul is referred to by his Hebrew name Saul ("God hears"). Paul was his second, Greek name. A brilliant young Pharisee, Paul was originally determined to stamp out Christianity. On his way to Damascus to arrest the Christians there, Jesus appeared to him in a vision and Paul was converted to Christianity. Very soon he started preaching the Christian message. Over the next thirty years he traveled all around the Greek-speaking world, specializing in preaching to non-Jews. He was thrown in prison several times, but kept in touch with his new churches by letter. Thirteen of his letters now form part of the New Testament.

## JOHN MARK

Meaning: *God is gracious*

Appears: *Acts 12, 13, 15; Col. 4; 2 Tim. 4; Philem. 24; 1 Pet. 5*

John Mark's mother had a large house in Jerusalem where the first Christians used to meet. John Mark went as a helper with Paul and Barnabas on their first missionary journey, but he lost heart halfway and went back to Jerusalem. He later went to Rome with Peter. John Mark is probably the author of Mark's Gospel.

## BARNABAS

Meaning: *Son of encouragement*

Appears: *Acts 4, 9, 11–15; 1 Cor. 9; Gal. 2; Col. 4*

One of the earliest converts to Christianity, Barnabas was a close friend of Paul, and traveled with him on his first missionary journey to Cyprus and Asia Minor. His real name was Joseph. "Barnabas" was a nickname the apostles gave him, because he was so good at teaching and encouraging people.

*Barnabas was a Greek-speaking Jew from Cyprus*

## PAUL'S MESSAGE

Missionaries like Paul felt that they had a unique message to pass on. They believed that Jesus died to save the world from evil, that he had risen from death to give people new life, and that God would give his Holy Spirit to all who believed.

### Paul's conversion

Paul discovered that he was to be a missionary while on the road to Damascus. Jesus appeared to him in a heavenly light, and told Paul to go out and preach all over the world. For three days he could not see and did not eat. Not all missionaries had a dramatic vision like Paul.

PAUL BECOMES A CHRISTIAN
*This painting by Francesco Mazzola (1503–40) shows Paul's conversion.*

### Paul's journeys

Paul made three long journeys from his home church in Antioch, Syria. Sometimes he went by ship, but he often walked from town to town, preaching on the way. He gave a famous sermon in Athens.

THE AGORA IN ATHENS
*Paul often sat here to discuss philosophy with the other teachers.*

## PHILIP

Meaning: *Lover of horses*
Appears: *Acts 6, 8, 21*

Philip's first job was distributing food to the poor in Jerusalem. He became a missionary and was the first to preach the good news in Samaria. On his way back to Jerusalem, Philip was taken by an angel to help an Ethiopian official who was confused by a passage in Isaiah. The official was so impressed, he asked to be baptized and became the first Ethiopian Christian.

*Philip explains the meaning to the Ethiopian*

## LUKE

Meaning: *unknown*
Appears: *Col. 4; 2 Tim. 4; Philem. 24*

Luke is the traditional author of Luke's Gospel and also the Acts of the Apostles. He was a good friend to Paul, and was with him when they experienced the storm and shipwreck (Acts 27). He was a Gentile and a doctor, and was able to care for Paul who suffered from a mysterious illness. Luke was the only person with Paul when he finally faced execution in Rome.

*LUKE*
*This page is from the 9th-century Irish Macdurnan Gospels.*

## SILAS

Meaning: *Woody*
Appears: *Acts 15, 16, 17, 18; 2 Cor. 1; 1 Thess. 1; 2 Thess. 1; 1 Pet. 5*

Silas traveled as a missionary with both Paul and Peter. He also sang hymns in jail with Paul during the earthquake in Philippi. Impressed by their faith, the jailer became a Christian. Peter described Silas as "a faithful brother."

*SILAS*

## TIMOTHY

Meaning: *One who honors God*
Appears: *Acts 16, 17; Rom. 16; 1 Cor. 4, 16; Phil. 1; Col. 1; 1 Thess. 3; 1 Tim. 1*

One of Paul's chief helpers, Timothy also went on missions of his own. Paul called him "my true son in the faith" and gave him advice in two letters in the New Testament.

*TITUS*
*A 14th-century Bible illustration*

## TITUS

Meaning: *Pleasant*
Appears: *2 Cor. 2, 7, 12; Gal. 2; 2 Tim. 4; Titus 1*

Titus was one of Paul's most trusted associates. Paul gave him an especially difficult task: to go ahead of Paul to the new church in Corinth, which was rebelling against Paul's leadership. Paul was delighted when Titus came back and said that the Corinthian Christians had now begun to soften their attitude. Later, Paul wrote Titus a letter (the book of Titus) that is preserved in the New Testament.

## EPAPHRODITUS

Meaning: *Handsome, charming*
Appears: *Phil. 2, 4*

A leader of the church in Philippi, Epaphroditus was sent by the church with a gift for Paul, who was under house arrest in Rome. Epaphroditus stayed to help Paul, but fell seriously ill. When he recovered, he returned home with Paul's letter to the Philippians.

## APOLLOS

Meaning: *Named after the Greek god Apollo*
Appears: *Acts 18, 19; 1 Cor. 1, 3, 4, 16; Titus 3*

A Jew from Alexandria in Egypt, Apollos was a missionary before he met Paul. He had been a disciple of John the Baptist and was a powerful preacher. Priscilla and Aquila helped Apollos to a clearer understanding of Jesus when they met him in Corinth.

## PHOEBE

Meaning: *Radiant*
Appears: *Rom. 16*

Phoebe was a church leader near Corinth. Unlike Jewish synagogues, many early Christian churches gave women leadership positions. Phoebe traveled to Rome, probably taking Paul's letter to the Romans.

## TYCHICHUS

Meaning: *Lucky*
Appears: *Acts 20; Eph. 6; Col. 4; 2 Tim. 4; Titus 3*

A Christian from Asia, Tychichus traveled with Paul to Jerusalem. He also took Paul's letters to the Ephesians and the Colossians to the churches there, and gave them news of Paul at the same time. Paul trusted him with other missions as well.

### SEE ALSO

✝ John the Baptist p 40
✝ Peter p 46
✝ Paul p 52
✝ Priscilla and Aquila p 56

# CHURCH MEMBERS AND OPPONENTS

S T. LUKE TELLS the story of the first Christians in the Acts of the Apostles. This provides a record of the first thirty years of the church and describes the work of the apostles as well as that of ordinary church members. It also gives an account of those who opposed Christianity and fought against the new faith.

*Ananias falls down dead*

## MATTHIAS

Meaning: *Gift of God*
Appears: *Acts 1*

After Judas Iscariot committed suicide, the remaining apostles decided to replace him. Of the two candidates, Matthias was chosen as the new apostle.

MATTHIAS

## ANANIAS

Meaning: *God is gracious*
Appears: *Acts 5*

Together with his wife Sapphira, Ananias joined the church in its earliest days. The love between the first Christians was so strong that they were willing to give up all their possessions if they were needed by other church members. Some brought very large gifts that they presented to the apostles to be distributed among the poor in Jerusalem. Ananias and Sapphira sold a field, but pretended they had sold it for less than the actual amount, and secretly kept the extra money for themselves. God told Peter what Ananias had done, so Peter confronted him. "You did not have to give the whole sum," he said, "but you have lied to the Holy Spirit!" As Peter spoke, Ananias collapsed and died.

## SAPPHIRA

Meaning: *Beautiful*
Appears: *Acts 5*

About three hours after her husband Ananias's death, Sapphira called on Peter the apostle, not knowing what had happened. Peter tested her by asking if the money was the total from the land sale, but she kept up the pretense about the value of their gift. She and Ananias wanted to be admired for making a greater sacrifice than they actually had. Peter knew how God would react, and warned her. It was too late – she collapsed and died. As a result, people inside and outside the church became very afraid, realizing that they could not be dishonest with God.

## THE FIRST MARTYR

I t was not long before the church mourned its first martyr – someone who gives their life for their faith. Stephen was the first of a long line of people who died for proclaiming their Christian beliefs.

**St. Stephen**
When Stephen was brought before the Sanhedrin, he made a long speech in his defense. As he finished, he had a vision of Jesus standing beside God. This incensed his enemies who stoned him to death. Before dying he said, "Lord, do not hold this sin against them."

*High Priest and members of the Sanhedrin*

DEATH OF ST. STEPHEN
*This painting is by Juan de Juanes (1523–79).*

**The Sanhedrin**
The Sanhedrin – from the Greek word for council – was the Jewish high court. It had seventy-one members, with chief priests, teachers of the law, and elders. New Testament members included Gamaliel, Caiaphas, and Nicodemus.

## STEPHEN

Meaning: *Crown*

Appears: *Acts 6, 7, 11, 22*

Stephen was one of seven young men chosen to organize help for the poor, and to distribute food in Jerusalem. He was a deep thinker and a gifted speaker, and was full of the Holy Spirit. He miraculously healed the sick, and argued powerfully with the Greek-speaking Jews, persuading many of them to become Christians. But opposition to him grew and his enemies accused him falsely before the Sanhedrin. He was wrongly convicted of blasphemy and stoned to death. He became the first Christian martyr.

## ANANIAS OF DAMASCUS

Meaning: *God is gracious*

Appears: *Acts 9*

One of the Christians in Damascus, Ananias was told by God to go to the house where Paul went after being blinded. Ananias knew that Paul had come to arrest all the Christians, but he went anyway. As he prayed, Paul's sight was restored.

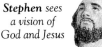

*Stephen sees a vision of God and Jesus*

## DORCAS (TABITHA)

Meaning: *Gazelle*

Appears: *Acts 9*

Dorcas lived in Joppa (modern Jaffa), where she was much loved for her many good works. One day she suddenly fell ill and died. Her distressed friends sent for Peter, who came and prayed beside the bed where she lay. As he prayed, her life returned and she sat up. Many of her friends, overjoyed by this miracle, became believers.

*Peter prays for Dorcas*

*Dorcas suddenly sits up in bed*

## SIMON THE TANNER

Meaning: *God hears*

Appears: *Acts 9, 10*

Tanners are people who treat the skins of animals to produce leather. They were generally shunned by strict Jews because of their contact with dead animals. Simon the Tanner must have been delighted when the great apostle Peter did not avoid him, but stayed at his home outside Joppa.

## CORNELIUS

Meaning: *unknown*

Appears: *Acts 10*

Cornelius was a Roman soldier stationed at Caesarea. He was a "God-fearer," the name given to Gentiles who joined the synagogue, seeking God. One day an angel appeared and told him to send for Peter. Cornelius gathered his friends and relatives to meet Peter. When he arrived, Cornelius knelt before him, but Peter said "I am only a man myself!" Then he told them about Jesus, and as he spoke the Holy Spirit came upon Cornelius and his friends. They were baptized immediately, praising God.

*Cornelius kneels before the apostle Peter*

*RHODA, THE SERVANT*

## RHODA

Meaning: *Rose*

Appears: *Acts 12*

Rhoda worked in Mary's house. She was praying for Peter, who was in prison awaiting execution the next day. When Rhoda heard Peter's voice at the door she was so amazed that she forgot to let him in.

## MARY, MOTHER OF JOHN MARK

Meaning: *unknown*

Appears: *Acts 12*

Mary's house in Jerusalem was where church members met. According to tradition, the last supper took place there.

### SEE ALSO

✝ Nicodemus p 43
✝ Peter 46
✝ Caiaphas p 49
✝ Gamaliel p 49
✝ Paul p 52

*Simon envies Philip's power to heal*

## SIMON MAGUS
Meaning: *God hears (Simon); Sorcerer (Magus)*
Appears: *Acts 8*

Simon was a magician in Samaria. When Philip arrived there, Simon already had a large following of people who regarded him as a manifestation of God. Simon saw the miracles that Philip performed and recognized the great power behind them, so he became a Christian. However, he really only wanted the power, for which he offered money to Peter. Peter told him, "Your heart is not right before God!" According to tradition, Simon became even more famous, but he continued to value magic above true faith in God.

## ELYMAS
Meaning: *unknown*
Appears: *Acts 13*

Elymas was a Jewish magician, who had great influence with the Roman Governor of Cyprus, Sergius Paulus. When Paul arrived, and Sergius showed interest in the Christian message, Elymas saw his position threatened. In turn, Paul denounced Elymas as "a child of the devil," and he was struck with temporary blindness. Sergius Paulus was so amazed that he became a Christian.

## JUDAS BARSABBAS
Meaning: *Praised*
Appears: *Acts 15*

A member of the Jerusalem church, Judas took an important letter to the church in Antioch. Church officials had been discussing whether Gentile believers should be circumcised. The apostles met in Jerusalem to talk about this, and sent their answer through Judas and Silas: no, they need not be circumcised.

*Judas carries the apostles' reply back to Antioch*

## LYDIA
Meaning: *Lady from Lydia*
Appears: *Acts 16*

Lydia lived in Philippi, where she had a successful business selling purple cloth from her hometown of Thyatira. She was a Gentile, seeking God by worshiping at the Jewish prayer center. It was here she met Paul and his fellow missionaries. Lydia responded warmly to the Gospel, and she and all her family and workers were baptized. She immediately invited Paul and his friends to stay in her home.

*LYDIA*

## JASON
Meaning: *God saves*
Appears: *Acts 17*

Jason was a Jew, living in Thessalonika. Paul came to the synagogue there and convinced Jason and others of the truth of the Christian message. But some of the Jews were jealous and had Jason thrown into prison.

*Elymas is no longer able to see*

## STEPHANAS
Meaning: *Crown*
Appears: *1 Cor. 1, 16*

Stephanas and his household were the first people to become Christians during Paul's ministry in Achaia, the Greek province that included Corinth where he lived. Stephanas and his household were baptized by Paul. As the church grew, Stephanas began to care for new Christians himself. Paul always retained a special affection for Stephanas, and was delighted when he visited him in Ephesus.

## PRISCILLA
Meaning: *Ancient*
Appears: *Acts 18; Rom. 16; 1 Cor. 16; 2 Tim. 4*

Priscilla and Aquila, her husband, worked closely with Paul, and even risked their lives for him. They became loved and respected in many churches in Greece and Asia Minor. Unusually, Priscilla's name is often mentioned before Aquila's.

## AQUILA
Meaning: *Eagle*
Appears: *Acts 18; Rom. 16; 1 Cor. 16; 2 Tim. 4*

Aquila was a Jew from Pontus who ran a successful business in Rome. When Claudius expelled the Jews from Rome, he and his wife traveled to Corinth where they met Paul and became Christians. They became good friends with Paul, and accompanied him when he moved to Ephesus.

## DEMETRIUS

Meaning: *Servant of Demeter*

Appears: *Acts 19*

Demetrius was a silversmith in Ephesus. He made a good living selling silver images of the goddess Artemis, whose temple in Ephesus was visited by many people. Paul's ministry in Ephesus began to affect sales because people stopped buying idols. Demetrius persuaded his fellow craftsmen that the honor of Artemis was under threat. They started shouting, "Great is Artemis" and soon the city was in an uproar. Paul tried to speak to the crowd, but his friends stopped him. In the end, the city clerk quelled the riot.

## JOHN'S REVELATION

The Book of Revelation, the last book in the Bible, was written by John – probably not the apostle, but another disciple with a powerful gift of prophecy. John's vision is a celebration of Jesus' triumph over death.

### At Ephesus
An angel of God told John to write his visions down and send them to the seven main churches in Asia. John's first letter was addressed to the church in Ephesus.

*TEMPLE IN EPHESUS, TURKEY*

### John's Revelations
While imprisoned on the Greek island of Patmos, John had an amazing series of visions. First he saw the risen Christ, then John himself was called up to heaven where he saw events on Earth, both present and future.

*JOHN'S VISION
This painting is by Hans Memling (c.1433–94).*

*Demetrius makes silver images of the goddess Artemis*

*The city clerk suggests the craftsmen go to court*

## EUTYCHUS

Meaning: *Lucky*

Appears: Acts 20

On his last evening in Troas, Macedonia, Paul was preaching and talking with a group of Christians. The heat from several lamps and the stuffy atmosphere in the room led Eutychus, a young man, to fall asleep on a third-floor window ledge. Unfortunately, Eutychus fell as he slept, and was feared for dead as he lay on the ground. Everyone rushed downstairs and Paul embraced Eutychus. "Do not worry," he said, "he is alive!" Eutychus soon regained consciousness.

*Eutychus falls asleep as Paul is talking*

## AGABUS

Meaning: *Desire*

Appears: Acts 11, 21

Agabus was a Christian prophet from Jerusalem. He predicted the famine that caused great hardship in Jerusalem. He also met Paul during Paul's last journey to Jerusalem and predicted that he would be imprisoned by the Romans there. Paul's friends tried to persuade him not to continue but they failed. Agabus's prophecy came true.

## PHILEMON

Meaning: *Kiss*

Appears: *Philemon*

Philemon was a wealthy Christian of Colossae, who was converted by the apostle Paul. Philemon had a slave named Onesimus who ran away but became a Christian when he met Paul. Paul sent him back to his master, asking Philemon to receive him as a "beloved brother."

### SEE ALSO
✝ Philip p 47
✝ Sergius Paulus p 51

# MORE PEOPLE IN THE BIBLE

THESE PAGES provide an introduction to more of the people who appear in the Bible, but who are not described in the main text entries. They are listed in alphabetical order.

*Ahijah tears his new cloak into twelve pieces*

## ABIJAH
Appears: *1 Kings 15*
The son of King Rehoboam of Judah, Abijah reigned only briefly after his father.

## ADONIRAM
Appears: *1 Kings 4, 5, 12*
Adoniram was in charge of forced labor under King Solomon and his son Rehoboam. Eventually the people rebelled and stoned Adoniram to death.

## ADONIZEDEK
Appears: *Josh. 10*
Adonizedek was king of Jerusalem at the time the Israelites entered the promised land. He fought against them but was defeated.

## AENEAS
Appears: *Acts 9*
Aeneas had been paralyzed for eight years when Peter arrived in his hometown of Lydda. "Jesus Christ heals you," said Peter – and Aeneas got up. This had quite an effect on the townspeople.

## AGUR
Appears: *Prov. 30*
Agur was a wise man, some of whose sayings have been collected in the book of Proverbs.

## AHIJAH
Appears: *1 Kings 11*
This prophet prompted Jeroboam to lead a rebellion against Solomon by tearing his cloak into twelve pieces (symbolizing the twelve tribes) and giving Jeroboam ten of them.

## AHIMELECH
Appears: *1 Sam. 21, 22*
The priest at Nob, Ahimelech helped David flee from Saul. Saul then ordered the execution of David and his family, as well as the population of the town.

## AHINOAM
Appears: *1 Sam. 14*
Married to King Saul, Ahinoam had three sons and two daughters.

## AHINOAM
Appears: *1 Sam. 25, 27, 30; 2 Sam. 3*
David's first wife, Ahinoam was the mother of his son Amnon.

## AHITHOPHEL
Appears: *2 Sam. 15–17*
David's chief adviser, Ahithophel joined Absalom's rebellion against David. He committed suicide when Absalom rejected his advice.

## ALEXANDER
Appears: *2 Tim. 4*
"Alexander the metalworker did me great harm," says Paul. We do not know what Alexander did, but perhaps he behaved like Demetrius the silversmith.

## ANDRONICUS AND JUNIA
Appear: *Rom. 16*
In his list of greetings in Romans, Paul mentions this husband and wife who were "outstanding among the apostles," and had been Christians longer than him.

## ARISTARCHUS
Appears: *Acts 19, 20, 27; Col. 4; Philemon*
One of Paul's team of missionary helpers, Aristarchus was from Thessalonika. He was shipwrecked and imprisoned with Paul.

## ASAHEL
Appears: *2 Sam. 2*
The brother of David's army commanders Joab and Abishai, Asahel was murdered by Abner, the commander of Saul's army.

## ASAPH
Appears: *Psalms 73, 74*
Asaph was a singer in the temple in Jerusalem; he wrote many of the psalms in the Bible.

## AZARIAH
Appears: *2 Kings 15; Isa. 6*
Azariah (or Uzziah) was king of Judah. He suffered from leprosy, so his son Jotham acted as regent most of the time.

## BAASHA
Appears: *1 Kings 15, 16*
Baasha assassinated Nadab, king of Israel, and took the throne. He reigned for twenty-four years.

## BARUCH
Appears: *Jer. 32, 36, 43, 45*
Jeremiah dictated his prophecies to Baruch, who read them out in the temple. When King Jehoiakim destroyed the scroll, Baruch wrote them out again.

## BEN-AMMI
Appears: *Gen. 19*
Ben-Ammi was one of Lot's two sons. He was the founder of the tribe of Ammonites.

## BERA
Appears: *Gen. 14*
Bera was the king of Sodom, where Lot lived. Abraham rescued Bera and Lot when they were captured by Kedorlaomer.

## BETHUEL
Appears: *Gen. 22, 24, 28*
The father of Rebekah, Bethuel was Abraham's nephew.

## BLASTUS
Appears: *Acts 12*
When the people of Tyre and Sidon tried to win favor with Herod Agrippa I, they secured the help of Blastus, his chief steward.

## CHLOE
Appears: *1 Cor. 1*
Chloe was a leading member of the church in Corinth.

## DAMARIS
Appears: *Acts 17*
An aristocratic Athenian lady, Damaris became a Christian after hearing Paul speak before the Areopagus – the supreme court in Athens.

## DEBORAH
Appears: *Gen. 24, 35*
Deborah was Rebekah's old nurse who traveled with her when she went to marry Isaac.

## DEMAS
Appears: *Col. 4; Philemon; 2 Tim. 4*
One of Paul's team of missionary helpers, Demas eventually gave up and deserted him "because he loved this world," as Paul said.

## DIONYSIUS
Appears: *Acts 17*
A member of the supreme court in Athens, Dionysius became a Christian after hearing Paul speak.

## DIOTREPHES
Appears: *3 John*
Diotrephes caused trouble in one of the churches for which John was responsible. He refused to accept John's teaching and authority. John wrote to his friend Gaius about it.

## DOEG
Appears: *1 Sam. 21, 22*
Doeg betrayed Ahimelech, the priest, to Saul for helping David escape. As punishment, Saul ordered Doeg to kill Ahimelech and his entire family.

## EBED-MELECH
Appears: *Jer. 38*
An Egyptian, Ebed-Melech gently lifted Jeremiah out of the punishment pit into which he had been thrown by his enemies.

## ELAH
Appears: *1 Kings 16*
Son of King Baasha, Elah reigned over Israel for only two years before he was assassinated by Zimri, one of his servants.

## ELDAD AND MEDAD
Appears: *Num. 11*
Two members of Moses's group of elders, they received the Holy Spirit and started prophesying.

## ELIAB
Appears: *1 Sam. 16, 17*
David's oldest brother, Eliab, together with two other brothers, Abinadab and Shammah, were soldiers in King Saul's army.

## ELIAKIM
Appears: *2 Kings 18, 19*
The palace administrator Eliakim was sent by King Hezekiah to confer with officials of King Sennacherib when he threatened to attack Jerusalem.

## ELIASHIB
Appears: *Neh. 3*
Eliashib was the high priest who helped Nehemiah build the walls of Jerusalem.

## ELIHU
Appears: *Job 32*
A fourth friend of Job, Elihu tried to set Job and his friends straight when they could not agree over the reasons for Job's sufferings.

## ELIPHAZ, BILDAD, AND ZOPHAR
Appear: *Job*
These three friends of Job came to comfort him when he lost everything. They each spoke to him in turn, but only managed to make him feel worse.

## EPAPHRAS
Appears: *Col. 1, 4; Philemon*
One of Paul's team of missionary helpers, Epaphras was from Colossae, and worked hard to build up the church there. When Paul wrote to the Colossians, Epaphras was in prison with him.

## EPHRON
Appears: *Gen. 23, 25, 49, 50*
Ephron owned the field in Machpelah that Abraham bought for the burial of his wife Sarah. Abraham was also buried there.

## ERASTUS
Appears: *Acts 19; 2 Tim. 4*
One of Paul's helpers, Erastus went on missions to preach and take care of the young churches.

## ERASTUS
Appears: *Rom. 16*
This Erastus was a prominent Christian in Corinth. A pavement laid by him and inscribed with his name has been discovered by archaeologists.

## EUODIA AND SYNTYCHE
Appear: *Phil. 4*
These two women in the church in Philippi had fallen out with each other. Paul appealed to them to "agree in the Lord."

## FORTUNATUS AND ACHAICUS
Appear: *1 Cor. 16*
Messengers from the Corinthian church, they came with their friend Stephanas, to visit Paul in Ephesus. Paul was delighted.

## GAIUS
Appears: *1 Cor. 1*
Gaius was one of the first Christians in Corinth to be baptized by Paul.

## GAIUS
Appears: *Acts 19, 20*
One of Paul's team of missionary helpers, Gaius was from Derbe in Asia Minor. He was nearly killed in the riot in Ephesus.

## GEDALIAH
Appears: *2 Kings 25; Jer. 40, 41*
The king of Babylon appointed Gedaliah – a Jew – to govern Judah for him after he had destroyed Jerusalem. Gedaliah was soon assassinated.

## GEHAZI
Appears: *2 Kings 4, 5, 8*
The servant of the prophet Elisha, Gehazi tried to swindle Naaman, the Syrian officer who came to Elisha for help. Elisha dismissed him.

## GERSHOM
Appears: *Exod. 2, 18*
Moses's son Gershom was looked after by his grandfather Jethro while Moses went to bring the Israelites out of Egypt.

## GOMER
Appears: *Hosea 1, 3*
Wife of Hosea the prophet, Gomer was the prostitute who God told Hosea to marry so that he would understand God's pain at Israel's unfaithfulness.

## HADADEZER
Appears: *2 Sam. 8, 10*
Hadadezer was the Syrian king of Zobah. When David defeated him, Syria submitted to David and started paying tribute.

## HAMOR
Appears: *Gen. 34*
The father of Shechem, Hamor tried unsuccessfully to negotiate peace with Jacob's sons.

## HANAMEL
Appears: *Jer. 32*
Jeremiah bought a field from his cousin Hanamel when the Babylonian army besieged Jerusalem. It was a symbol of hope.

## HANANIAH
*Appears: Jer. 28*
This false prophet opposed Jeremiah and his message of coming judgment. Jeremiah accurately foretold Hananiah's imminent death.

## HARAN
Appears: *Gen. 11*
Haran was Abraham's brother and the father of Lot. Abraham named a city after him.

## HEBER
Appears: *Judg. 4*
The husband of Jael, Heber murdered Sisera, an army commander from Hazor. She was descended from Moses's father-in-law.

*Jannes and Jambres watch as their snake is swallowed up*

## HEGAI
Appears: *Esther 2*
Hegai was in charge of King Xerxes' harem. He looked after Esther when she arrived to become the king's new wife.

## HOPHNI AND PHINEAS
Appear: *1 Sam. 1, 2, 4*
The wicked sons of Eli, Hophni and Phineas abused their office as priests and brought ruin on Eli's house and on Israel.

## HUSHAI
Appears: *2 Sam. 16, 17*
Hushai, David's old friend and adviser, pretended to join Absalom's rebellion but secretly reported his plans to David.

## ISHBI-BENOB
Appears: *2 Sam. 21*
This giant was related to Goliath. When David was older, Ishbi-Benob nearly killed him in a battle. Abishai rescued him.

## ISHMAEL
Appears: *2 Kings 25; Jer. 40, 41*
Jeremiah tells the story of the assassination of Gedaliah, the governor of Judah, by a young rebel called Ishmael.

## JAIR
Appears: *Judg. 10*
A minor judge who led Israel for twenty-two years just before the time of Jephthah.

## JANNES AND JAMBRES
Appear: *Exod. 7, 8; 2 Tim. 3*
These are the traditional names of the Egyptian magicians who opposed Moses and Aaron.

*Aaron throws his staff down before Pharaoh and it turns into a snake*

*Jochebed hides her baby Moses in the reeds of the River Nile*

## JEHOAHAZ
Appears: *2 Kings 13*
The son of King Jehu of Israel, Jehoahaz reigned for seventeen years, but during this time Israel fell under the power of Syria.

## JEHOAHAZ
Appears: *2 Kings 23*
This Jehoahaz, son of King Josiah, reigned for only three months before being carried off to Egypt as a prisoner by Pharaoh Neco.

## JEHOIAKIM
Appears: *2 Kings 23, 24*
King of Judah for eleven years, Jehoiakim paved the way for the Babylonian invasion with some very unwise actions and bad rule.

## JEHORAM
Appears: *2 Kings 8*
The son of Jehoshaphat, king of Judah, Jehoram reigned for eight years. His queen was Athaliah, the daughter of Ahab, who killed her grandsons.

## JEHOSHEBA
Appears: *2 Kings 11*
The brave daughter of Athaliah, Jehosheba hid baby Joash, the heir to the throne, for six years until her mother was executed and Joash became king.

## JERUB-BAAL
Appears: *Judg. 6*
This was the name given to Gideon after he smashed the altar of the god Baal in his father's garden. It means "let Baal fight."

## JOBAB
Appears: *Josh. 11*
Jobab, king of Madon, joined forces with Jabin, king of Hazor, to fight the Israelites when they entered the promised land.

## JOCHEBED
Appears: *Exod. 2, 6*
Moses' mother, she hid her baby when the Egyptians demanded that all baby boys were to die.

## JONATHAN AND AHIMAAZ
Appear: *2 Sam. 15, 17, 18; 1 Kings 1*
The two sons of Zadok and Abiathar, the priests, acted as secret runners taking messages about Absalom's plans to David.

## JOSEPH BARSABBAS
Appears: *Acts 1*
Joseph was the suggested replacement for the disciple Judas, who committed suicide after betraying Jesus.

## JOTHAM
Appears: *2 Kings 15*
The son of King Azariah of Judah, Jotham was a good ruler after his father's death.

## JOTHAM
Appears: *Judg. 9*
Gideon's youngest son, Jotham was the only one to escape when all his older brothers were murdered by their half-brother Abimelech.

## KILION
Appears: *Ruth 1*
This son of Elimelech and Naomi married Orpah, the Moabite. Kilion died suddenly, just as his father.

## KISH
Appears: *1 Sam. 9*
The father of Saul, who became the first king of Israel. Saul was looking for Kish's lost donkeys when Samuel found Saul and anointed him king.

## LOIS AND EUNICE
Appear: *2 Tim. 1*
These two women are the grandmother and mother of Timothy. Paul thanks God for their "sincere faith."

## LUCIUS
Appears: *Acts 13*
Lucius was a North African teacher at the church in Antioch from where Paul and Barnabas set off on their first journey.

## MAHER-SHALAL-HASHBAZ
Appears: *Isa. 8*
Isaiah the prophet gave his son this long name, which means "quick to the plunder, swift to the spoil." His name was to remind the Israelites of God's coming judgment.

## MAHLON
Appears: *Ruth 1*
One of the sons of Elimelech and Naomi, Mahlon married Ruth, the young Moabite girl. He then died suddenly, just as his father.

## MANAEN
Appears: *Acts 13*
Manaen was a leading member of the Antioch church where Paul was nurtured. Manaen was an aristocrat who had been brought up with the Herod family.

## MERAB
Appears: *1 Sam. 18*
Saul promised his older daughter, Merab, in marriage to David, but then broke his promise.

## MERODACH-BALADAN
Appears: *2 Kings 20; Isa. 39*
Hezekiah foolishly showed all his treasures to the officials of this Babylonian king. This reminded the Babylonians that Jerusalem was worth capturing.

## MILCAH
Appears: *Gen. 11, 22*
Abraham's niece, Milcah was married to his brother Nahor.

## MOAB
Appears: *Gen. 19*
Moab was one of Lot's two sons. It was from him that the tribe of Moabites were descended.

## NABAL
Appears: *1 Sam. 25*
Nabal was the first husband of David's wife Abigail, and was rude and ungrateful to David and his men. He died of shock when his wife told him that he had almost been murdered by David and his men.

## NABOTH
Appears: *1 Kings 21*
Naboth owned a vineyard near King Ahab's palace. Jezebel bribed two men to accuse Naboth of blasphemy and had him killed. She took the vineyard for her husband Ahab. Elijah pronounced God's judgment on them for this crime.

## NADAB AND ABIHU
Appear: *Exod. 24, 28; Lev. 10*
These sons of Aaron became priests with their father. They were murdered in the tabernacle when they invented new rituals.

## NADAB
Appears: *1 Kings 14, 15*
Son of King Jeroboam, Nadab only reigned for two years after his father. He was assassinated by Baasha.

## NAHASH
Appears: *1 Sam. 11*
This wicked Ammonite king threatened to blind all the people of Jabesh Gilead. King Saul rescued them.

## NAHUM
Appears: *Nahum*
One of the minor prophets, Nahum's prophecy of judgment on Nineveh, capital of the Assyrian Empire, is recounted in the Bible.

## NEBUZARADAN
Appears: *2 Kings 25*
Commander of the Babylonian army, he ordered the destruction of Jerusalem in 587 BC.

## NYMPHA
Appears: *Col. 4*
A leading member of the church in Colossae, Nympha had a church meeting in her house.

## OBADIAH
Appears: *Obadiah*
A minor prophet whose prophecy of judgment on the nation of Edom appears in the Bible.

## OBADIAH
Appears: *1 Kings 18*
Chief administrator of Ahab's palace, Obadiah used palace resources of bread and water to keep alive one hundred prophets during a famine.

## OBED
Appears: *Ruth 4*
The baby son born to Ruth and Boaz, Obed was the grandfather of King David.

## OG
Appears: *Num. 21; Deut; 3, Josh.12*
King of Bashan, Og tried to stop the Israelites from entering the promised land.

## OHOLIAB

Appears: *Exod. 31, 35, 36, 38*
Bezalel's assistant, he helped make all the furnishings and decorations for the tabernacle.

## ONESIMUS

Appear: *Philemon; Col. 4*
Onesimus was the slave who ran away from his Christian master, Philemon. When he met Paul, he became a Christian too. Paul sent him back with a wonderful letter, asking Philemon to receive Onesimus as a brother.

## ONESIPHORUS

Appears: *2 Tim. 1*
Onesiphorus tracked Paul down in the prisons in Rome and cared for him.

## ORPAH

Appears: *Ruth 1*
Orpah was one of Naomi's two widowed daughters-in-law. The other, Ruth, traveled with Naomi to Bethlehem, but Orpah stayed in her native Moab.

## PALTIEL

Appears: *1 Sam. 25; 2 Sam. 3*
When David fell out of favor with Saul and ran away, Saul gave his daughter Michal, David's wife, to Paltiel. Paltiel was sorry when David demanded her back.

## PEKAHIAH

Appears: *2 Kings 15*
The king of Israel for two years, Pekahiah was assassinated by Pekah, one of his officers, who then took the throne.

## PHYGELUS AND HERMOGENES

Appear: *2 Tim. 1*
These former friends of Paul did not stand by him when he was thrown into prison for being a Christian.

## REHUM

Appears: *Ezra 4*
Rehum was a local non-Jewish commander who tried to prevent the rebuilding of Jerusalem and the temple by Zerubbabel and Jeshua. For a while he was successful.

## REZIN

Appears: *2 Kings 16, Isa. 7*
Rezin was a king of Syria who conspired with Pekah, the king of Israel, to attack Judah and

Jerusalem. Their plans came to nothing, as Isaiah had prophesied.

## SCEVA

Appears: *Acts 19*
A Jewish chief priest, Sceva had seven sons, all of whom were exorcists in Ephesus. They used the name of Jesus in their exorcisms, even though they were not Christians.

## SERAIAH

Appears: *2 Kings 25*
Seraiah had the sad task of being the last high priest in Jerusalem before the exile. He saw the temple destroyed by the Babylonians.

## SHAPHAN

Appears: *2 Kings 22*
The secretary Shaphan read the book of God's Law to King Josiah. The reading had a profound effect on the king.

## SHECHEM

Appears: *Gen. 34*
Shechem the Canaanite prince raped Dinah, Jacob's daughter, then fell in love with her. Despite this, he was killed for his action.

## SHESHBAZZAR

Appears: *Ezra 1, 5*
The Persian governor in charge of Judah, Sheshbazzar had the job of bringing back to Jerusalem all the gold and silver articles taken away by King Neduchadnezzar.

## SHIMEI

Appears: *2 Sam. 16, 19*
Shimei cursed David repeatedly as he fled from Jerusalem before Absalom. Abishai wanted to kill Shimei but David stopped him. Later David forgave him.

## SIMEON

Appears: *Acts 13*
A leading member of the mixed church at Antioch in Syria. Simeon was also called Niger, meaning "black." Possibly he was one of the first African Christians.

## SOSTHENES

Appears: *Acts 18; 1 Cor. 1*
One of Paul's team of missionary helpers, Sosthenes was a Jew from Corinth. He helped Paul write his first letter to the church there.

## TATTENAI

Appears: *Ezra 5, 6*
Tattenai was governor of the Persian province of Trans-Euphrates, which included Judah. Instructed by King Darius, he supported the Jews in their rebuilding of the temple.

## TERTIUS

Appears: *Rom. 16*
Tertius the scribe wrote down the letter to the Romans as Paul dictated it. At the end of the letter Tertius sends his own greetings to the recipients.

## TERTULLUS

Appears: *Acts 24*
The lawyer Tertullus was hired by the Jewish authorities to present their case against Paul before Felix, the Roman governor.

## TOBIAH

Appears: *Neh. 2, 4, 6*
The associate of Sanballat, Tobiah organized opposition to Nehemiah's rebuilding project in Jerusalem.

## TROPHIMUS

Appears: *Acts 20, 21; 2 Tim. 4*
One of Paul's team of missionary helpers, Trophimus was a Gentile from Ephesus. He was the cause of a riot in Jerusalem, because some Jews thought that Paul had taken him into the temple.

## TYRANNUS

Appears: *Acts 19*
Tyrannus owned a lecture hall in Ephesus, where Paul held daily discussions to persuade people to become Christians.

## URIAH

Appears: *2 Sam. 11*
Uriah was the husband of Bathsheba. David arranged his murder so that he could have Bathsheba for himself.

## ZEBEDEE

Appears: *Matt.4; Luke 5; John 21*
The father of disciples James and John, Zebedee was a fisherman on Lake Galilee. His wife Salome was a follower of Jesus, and stood by the cross while Jesus died.

## ZELOPHEHAD

Appears: *Num. 27, 36; Josh. 17*
Zelophehad had five daughters – Mahlah, Noah, Hoglah, Milcah, and Tirzah – and no sons. The law was changed so that his daughters could inherit their father's estate.

## ZEPHANIAH

Appears: *Zephaniah*
One of the minor prophets, Zephaniah lived in the time of Josiah. The Bible includes his prophecy of judgment on Judah and the surrounding nations.

## ZIBA

Appears: *2 Sam. 9, 16, 19*
The servant of Saul, Ziba became chief administrator of Saul's estates for Mephibosheth, Jonathan's disabled son.

## ZIMRI

Appears: *1 Kings 16*
Zimri assassinated King Elah of Israel, and tried to take the throne. He committed suicide when he realized that the people did not want him.

*Nabal sends David's men away empty-handed*

# INDEX

# Acknowledgments

DK would like to thank the following: Cathy Edkins, Denise O'Brien, and Caroline Potts: picture research; Sarah Crouch, Robin Hunter: additional design; Hilary Bird: index; Lynn Bresler: proofreading. Additional artwork: Eric Thomas, Amy Burch.

**Photographic credits:**
c = center, l = left, r = right, t = top, b = bottom

**AKG London:** 9 cr, 21 cr, 31 bc, 37 bl, 44 b, 50 tl, 53 cr, 54 cr / Erich Lessing 5 cl, 9 bl, 20 bc, 42 br, 52 bc, 57 tr; **Ancient Art & Architecture Collection:** 15 br, 17 tr, 38 tl, 39 c / Julian Worker 37 cl / Ronald Sheridan 25 tc, 26 br, 29 bc, 31 t; **The Bridgeman Art Library:** Bible Society, London 6 cl / Bibliothèque Nationale, Paris 23 t / British Library, London 5 cr, 10 bc / Alberto Bruschi di Grassina Collection, Florence 37 tc / Duomo, Sienna 39 tl / Giraudon 22 bl / Lambeth Palace Library 25 tr, 53 bl / Louvre, Paris 51 cr / Monasterio de el Escorial, Spain 27 br / Musées Royaux des Beaux Arts de Belgique, Brussels 5 br / Museo d'Arte Moderno di Ca Pesaro, Venice 52 br / Private Collection 33 bl, 51 tc / Stapleton Collection 15 tc / Victoria & Albert Museum, London 4 tl / Peter Willi 12 br / Winchester Cathedral, Hampshire 25cl; **Sonia Halliday Photographs:** 10 bl, 44 tc, 57 tc / Sonia Halliday and Laura Lushington 43 bl; **Hutchison Picture Library:** / Moser 17 cr; **Zev Radovan:** 49 tr; **The Stock Market:** K Goebel 9 br; **Tony Stone Images:** 5 tl; **Telegraph Colour Library:** Patrick Ward 39 tr

# OIL TANKERS AT SEA

# GIANTS OF THE SEA

Oil tankers are the giants of the sea. The longest oil tankers are the length of the tallest buildings on Earth. These tankers can carry hundreds of thousands of tons of oil for thousands of miles over the world's oceans.

## Importance of Oil

Nearly every aircraft, car, truck, train, and ship can move only because their engines burn fuels made from oil. These fuels include gas, diesel, or **liquefied petroleum gas** (LPG). Oil is also used to make many products, from plastics to fertilizers.

## Need for Tankers

Oil is not distributed evenly around our planet. It is found only in certain types of rocks. The largest amounts of oil are located in the Middle East and parts of South America, Africa, Russia, the United States, and Europe. People in some regions use more oil than in others, so there is a need to transport oil or fuel products from place to place.

Globally, there are around 1.2 billion operational passenger cars. This number increases each year as the global population rises.

## Boats Are Best

Oil is heavy, and vast amounts are needed, so it is impractical to fly it between continents. Ocean barriers mean trains are unsuitable, too. A lot of oil needs to be pumped up from underground rocks beneath oceans. The best and cheapest way is to transport large amounts of oil on giant ships. Oil shipping makes up one-third of global ocean trade.

At sea, oil is pumped from underground rocks to oil platforms. Oil tankers then take it around the world to where it is needed.

# FOSSIL FUELS

Oil is a **fossil fuel** like coal and natural gas. Fossil fuels formed from the remains of ancient living things that became buried deep underground in mud. The mud eventually became layers of rock, and over millions of years, intense heat and **pressure** changed the remains into fuels. Oil formed from the remains of billions of tiny organisms that once lived in ancient seas.

# CONSTRUCTING OIL TANKERS

Oil tankers are built mostly from one of the strongest materials ever produced by people – steel.

## Steel to Ship

Steel is an **alloy**, or mix, of iron and carbon. Iron is strong and heavy but also brittle because of the carbon it normally contains after processing. Steel is made by reducing carbon, so that the metal becomes more flexible and easier to shape and bend without breaking.

Shipbuilders weld together plates of sheet steel to make curved pieces of the **hull**. The thickest sheets on the bottom of the ship are nearly 1 foot (30 cm) thick, but internal sheets are around 8 to 9 inches (20–23 cm). The inside is strengthened using many very strong steel **beams**, which span the length and width of the ship.

Welding is melting metal with intense heat, so that the pieces join together.

The problem with steel at sea is that the salt in seawater makes iron **rust** faster than it would in freshwater. Ocean ship hulls need to be covered with special rustproof coatings to slow down this process.

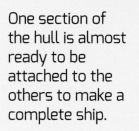

One section of the hull is almost ready to be attached to the others to make a complete ship.

## Tanker Modeling Kit

Most tankers are built by joining together sections, a little like a modeling kit. The sections may be built away from shipyards, and they contain the steel parts, piping, and electrical cables. Then, the shipbuilders lift sections into place using powerful cranes. They bolt or rivet the sections together, then connect the pipes and cables to form the complete hull. The ship is "floated," or placed in water for the first time, and then fitted with all of its other parts. These include the **deck**, the tall **bridge**, and the engines.

# BUILT FOR BULK

In a swimming pool, you will sink unless you swim, tread water, or wear a life preserver. An oil tanker is millions of times your size and **weight**, yet it can float. This is all because of **forces**.

## Forces

Forces are pushes and pulls that make things move. They work in pairs, so for every force in one direction, there is another force in the opposite direction. The two main forces on a tanker are **gravity** and **upthrust**. The weight of the tanker is caused by the downward pull of gravity from Earth on its great mass. Upthrust is the upward push on the tanker from seawater below its hull. Tankers float because the upthrust balances out the gravity.

## Taking Up Space

Imagine all the metal in a tanker squashed into a cube and placed on the sea. The cube has a high **density**, which is the amount of material packed into a given volume. Its density is greater than an equivalent cube of seawater, so it would sink fast. The same weight of metal in the shape of a tanker hull floats because it has a much lower density than the volume of seawater that it **displaces**.

## LOAD LINES

Every ship has a set of markings on the hull called load lines. These show how low the vessel can sit in the water before it is at risk of sinking. Load lines help workers avoid overloading ships. There are different lines for summer and winter because warm seawater has a higher density than cold seawater.

This giant tanker floats on a river to bring oil inland from the sea.

# TANKER POWER

Oil tankers can move forward because of a force called **thrust**. This is the push of a **propeller** powered by its engine. On such massive ships, the propellers and engines need to be very big.

## How Propellers Work

Propellers are a set of blades, usually four to six arranged in a ring. The alloy propellers on an oil tanker can be as large as tens of feet across. They can weigh many tons. Each blade is curved. Spinning the blades in one direction makes the curved blades push at the water they meet. Together, they produce a push at right angles away from the way it is spinning. The force of water backward from the ship creates an equal and opposite force from the water behind the ship. This pushes the boat forward in the water.

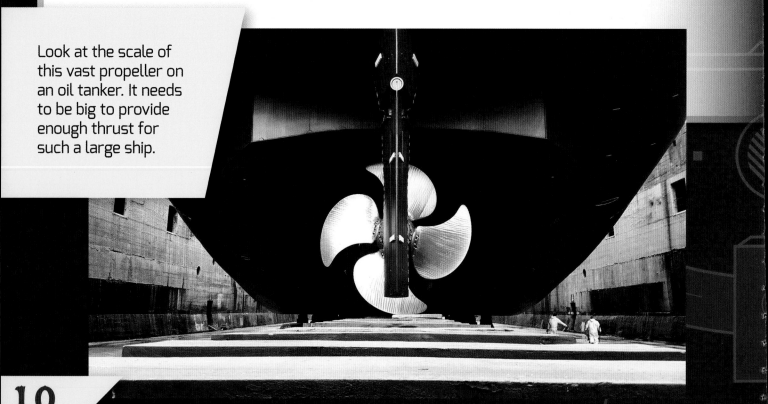

Look at the scale of this vast propeller on an oil tanker. It needs to be big to provide enough thrust for such a large ship.

## Big Engines

An oil tanker has a large room inside for its massive engine. The engine can be the size of an average house. Unsurprisingly, tanker engines are fuel guzzlers. At full speed, one of these can use more than 100 tons (91 tonnes) of fuel a day. There is room on a tanker to store the fuel.

The engine operates to make sure the tanker's propellers rotate at about 80 to 100 turns every minute. Any faster, and there would be little extra speed but more fuel use and wear on the blades. Any slower, and the oil would take too long to reach its destination.

## TANKER SPEED

Oil tanker engines are designed to propel the ship at an average speed of 15 knots. This is about 17 miles per hour (27 km/h).

11

# ON THE MOVE

When it is time for an oil tanker to leave the harbor, it often has the assistance of a tugboat or two. These powerful short boats attach to the tanker with strong ropes. They help pull and guide the ship to deeper, open water, where it can get its engine up to speed and start its journey.

## Big and Slow

Tankers have wide, long hulls because these displace more water than narrower, longer hulls. This enables them to carry heavy cargoes. The downside of being able to float great weight is the force called **drag**. This is the backward force of the seawater on the hull that opposes its thrust forward. Drag is greater on a large surface than a small surface. Tankers can unbalance the pair of forces to overcome drag and move forward only by having giant engines.

It takes an extra push from tugboats to shift massive oil tankers around in harbors.

## At Sea

Over its lifetime, a ship will encounter millions of waves. Tankers have very long hulls. Since large waves move along the length of a tanker, the center of this heavy ship is designed to bend up and down to cope with the waves' forces.

Oil tankers maneuver using giant **rudders** behind their propellers. These deflect the force of the water from the propeller to turn the ship. The process is slow because of the ship's length. A 500-foot (152 m), 8,000-ton (7,257 tonne) ship needs 1,584 feet (483 m) to turn around completely. Slowing to a stop can take 5 miles (8 km).

Waves make a tanker pitch up and down. When it dips at the front, waves crash over the deck.

## TAKE A BOW

Beneath the waterline, a tanker has a rounded lump sticking out. This bulbous **bow** calms the effect of waves hitting the bow. This improves comfort for the crew and stops the heavy ship from bouncing up and down violently.

13

# PARTS
# OF A TANKER

The most obvious thing about an oil tanker is that most of its length is a flat deck. Under the deck are the enormous spaces in which to store oil or fuels.

## Oil Tanks

A tanker usually has between 8 and 12 oil tanks. Each one is split into separate compartments because of the major strengthening steel beams running across and along the inside of the ship. In the event of a collision that causes a spill or fire in one tank, the other tanks will not be affected.

## OIL HEATERS

Many oil tankers have **pumps** that move oil from tanks past heaters. They do this because in cold conditions, oil becomes thicker and more difficult to pump out of the ship. Warming the oil makes it flow better.

The long pipes on top of a tanker deck carry fuel in and out of the tanks. Sailors sometimes use bicycles to travel the tanker's deck because it is so long.

# From the Top Down

The tanker's bridge is the tallest part of the ship, and it has the best view. At the top, the control room contains the equipment to steer, change speed, and navigate the ship. There are radios and computers to communicate with ports and other ships. Underneath, stairways lead to the crew's living quarters. These include spaces to sleep, washrooms, kitchens, and lounges where people can relax. An average oil tanker may have a total crew of 24, from the captain who is responsible for the ship and its safety, to engineers who work to maintain the ship's machinery.

Deeper still in the ship is the engine room. This contains the main engine for thrust and smaller engines used to supply electricity to the ship. This power is used, for example, to operate **winches** that lower and raise the giant anchors. The ship needs anchors to hold itself still when pausing during long journeys.

Wide pieces on either side of the bridge allow the crew to visualize the width of the tanker. This is important when maneuvering close to harbors and other ships.

NO SMOKING

# LOADING UP

Half of all oil tanker voyages are to destinations where they will load up with oil or fuels. The destinations include places where there are oil platforms. Oil platforms are structures with massive, hollow drills that pierce holes in underwater rocks and bring **crude oil** to the surface. They also include **refineries**, which are special chemical factories that convert crude oil into gas, diesel, and other oil products.

## Crude Oil Depots

Tankers can sometimes stop near platforms to load oil through pipes. However, it is tricky for tankers to get close to some oil platforms, especially in deep oceans with giant waves. They often get oil from floating depots called **FPSOs**, which are tethered to the seafloor. These are big storage tanks that contain the crude oil pumped from several platforms. Some FPSOs are old tankers that are no longer used to transport oil.

## Oil In, Gas and Water Out

Pumping in oil starts slowly at low pressure. This ensures that all connections are secure. As the space in the tank fills, this pushes out oil **vapor** from the tank. In small quantities, this is sometimes released into the atmosphere, or it is piped away for storage or conversion into fuel.

Many tankers empty of oil carry water in spaces called **ballast** tanks. The water adds weight to make the tanker sit low enough in the sea to handle properly during voyages to oil depots. As oil is pumped into tanks, ballast water is pumped out to control the tanker's weight.

# CONTROLLED MOVEMENT

When moving close to FPSOs or harbors, many tankers use **bow thrusters**. These are electrical propellers that point outward from the bow. They slowly push the tip of the bow left or right.

This boom from the oil platform is holding out the pipes to carry crude oil onto the tankers.

# UNLOADING

Unloading oil from a tanker is the reverse process of loading up. Great care needs to be taken to ensure the safety of the ship and its crew.

## Pumps On

The pumps on tankers can clear oil and fuels from tanks at a rate of around 450 cubic yards per hour (344 m³/h). Individual tanks have to be emptied at the same time and in the right order. The reason for this is that if the ship became too empty and light at one end or one side, it could become unstable in the water. This would put it at risk of **capsizing**.

Radar machines inside the tanks automatically check the levels of oil. Signals from these machines are transmitted to the computer on the bridge of the tanker, where the crew can control the oil levels throughout the whole ship.

Crude oil is unloaded into a tank. This raw material is needed in refineries to make fuels and other products.

The bulbous bow is obvious on this tanker because it is high in the water after the cargo has been unloaded at a refinery.

## Tank Clearing

After unloading the cargo, the tanks often need to be cleaned out. This prevents the next cargo from being **contaminated** by the previous one. It also allows inspectors to check for any possible leaks or damage, such as rusting, which could make the transportation of oil or fuels unsafe.

Contaminants inside the walls of a tank can include traces of diesel and grubby solids from crude oil. Tanks are washed using high-pressure, hot water sprays. The oily water is then pumped out of the tanks for safe disposal. The crew may then need to use mops, buckets, sponges, and rags to completely clean and dry the tanks.

## FUEL VAPORS

Vapors remaining in tanks are pushed out by blowing fresh air into the tank. Inspectors use handheld devices to check whether the tank is vapor-free before getting inside to check. They do this because, otherwise, their movements could accidentally cause a vapor explosion.

# CRUDE TANKERS

The tankers that transport crude oil from oil fields to refineries are called crude tankers. These are the largest tankers on the oceans.

## Types of Crude Tanker

Crude tankers carry a maximum weight of 55,000 to 450,000 tons (49,895–408,233 tonnes) of oil, including any cargo, such as ship fuel, provisions, and crew. The smallest crude tankers are the Panamax type. They get their name from having a width, depth, and length capable of traveling through the Panama Canal. The Panama Canal is a waterway in central America that links the Atlantic and Pacific Ocean. The biggest crude tankers are enormous supertankers.

## Ocean Highways

Crude tankers follow the same ocean routes from oil fields to refineries. Like other large ships, tankers move in shipping lanes, which are a little like ocean highways. They have northbound and southbound lanes, each 1 mile (2 km) wide with a safety gap of 3 miles (5 km) in between lanes to avoid collisions.

The most commonly used crude oil shipping lanes start in the Middle East. Some routes lead to the Americas around the bottom of Africa, some head to Asia, and others head to Europe via the Suez Canal.

## Never Empty!

The owners of crude tankers do not make money on the return legs from refineries, since their ships are empty. Some earn money by filling the spaces with heavy goods, such as iron ore, from nearby ports instead.

## NO COATING

Crude tankers have plain steel oil tanks with no special coating. Special coatings are unnecessary because crude oil does not cause **corrosion** of the metal as many other fuels do.

A small Handysize tanker is ideal for getting crude oil along narrow channels to customers.

NO SMOKING

SAFETY FIRST

# SUPERTANKERS

This supertanker is docking in Rotterdam, Netherlands. Rotterdam is one of the few ports big enough to fit them.

Supertankers are crude tankers that can carry more than the weight of the Empire State Building on each voyage. They have decks the size of four football fields.

## Very Large or Ultra Large

Supertankers come in two sizes – very large and ultra large. Very large crude carriers, or VLCCs, can carry between 180,000 and 320,000 tons (163,290– 291,000 tonnes) of crude oil. They are usually up to around 1,000 feet (305 m) long.

Ultra-large crude carriers, or ULCCs, can carry 320,000 to 500,000 tons (291,000–453,592 tonnes). They are generally longer and deeper than VLCCs, so they sit lower in the water. They are also so vast that they are slower and trickier to maneuver. For this reason, they can use only harbors specially built to fit them. Such harbors are found at just a few ports, including Rotterdam in the Netherlands and Singapore in Southeast Asia.

# Biggest Tankers

Today, the biggest tankers are the TI Europe and TI Oceania. These giants of the sea are 1,200 feet (366 m) long and 223 feet (68 m) wide. They can carry 441,000 tons (400,068 tonnes) of oil. The ships are painted white. This is because white reflects sunlight and helps keep the deck and the oil on board cool. Then oil evaporates into the atmosphere.

## RECORD BREAKER

The longest ship ever built was the *Mont*, which was also known as the *Jahre Viking* and *Knock Nevis*. It was 1,400 feet (427 m) long, 226 feet (69 m) wide, and could carry 564,000 tons (511, 652 tonnes) of oil. The *Mont* was slow and so vast that it risked running aground on some routes. It was broken up for scrap metal in 2009, and only the 36-ton (33 tonne) anchor remains. This anchor is on display at a boat museum in Hong Kong, China.

Look at the difference in size between the supertanker in the middle and the smaller oil tanker on the right.

# PRODUCT TANKERS

Product tankers carry fuels and other oil products from refineries to places where they can be used and sold.

## Tanks

One of the main differences between crude tankers and product tankers is that product storage tanks are coated with special paints to prevent the products from damaging the ships. Product tankers often carry several different types of products, and they have separate pipe systems to prevent them from contaminating each other when loading and unloading.

## Gases Inside

Many liquid oil products are difficult to burn, but their vapors are highly explosive when they mix with the oxygen found in air. Product tankers have systems to prevent the buildup of dangerous amounts of vapors. Gases that do not burn, called inert gases, are mixed into air to reduce the proportion of oxygen. This "safer" air is then pumped into tanks, so that the vapors cannot explode.

Product tankers are often smaller than crude tankers.

## Product Demand

There is global demand for products such as jet fuel for airplanes and gasoline for cars, so product tankers are always busy. Most product tankers travel coastal, shallower waters and move inland up rivers to reach their varied destinations from refineries. Tankers unload to storage tanks at destination ports, and tanker trucks and trains deliver fuels to users.

However, some product tankers travel across oceans. For example, a lot of diesel is produced in US refineries, and large amounts of gasoline are refined in Europe. These fuels are shipped across the oceans between the two regions to meet demand from users.

Some product tankers have large spherical tanks. These are used to safely transport LPG.

ARCTIC PRINCESS

## NAVAL OILERS

The navy operates some product tankers called naval oilers. Naval oilers are used to refuel aircraft carriers and warships while they are moving along. Refueling while underway avoids delays going into ports, so that naval missions are not interrupted.

# SAFER TANKERS

A world without oil tankers would grind to a halt. That is because tankers deliver the fuels that allow people to get around and travel. Like all ships, tankers sometimes have accidents. That is why they have safety equipment and designs to make them safer.

## Falling to Safety

Crew can escape an oil tanker that is sinking or on fire by falling to safety aboard its lifeboat. This is often located on a ramp at the **stern** of the ship near the bridge. The lifeboat is designed to protect people inside from the impact.

## Oil Spills

Oil tanker hulls can rip open when the tankers run aground or collide with other boats. When crude oil spills into the oceans, it causes pollution. It can poison sea creatures or coat coasts with a black, sticky mess that is very difficult to clean up.

A tanker lifeboat free-falls to the water tens of feet below.

Oil and fuels are highly flammable, so regular inspections are needed to make sure that they are safely stored and transported.

## Preventing Oil Spills

Oil tankers have a duty to be as safe as possible to prevent harming the oceans. They have various design features to help prevent oil spills:

- Double hulls: All new tankers have two hulls, one inside the other. If the outer skin is broken and seawater gets in, the ship will not sink.
- Protective ballasts: Ballast tanks are positioned at the bow and other places on a ship most likely to be involved in any collision. That means water, rather than oil, is spilled.
- Double controls: Tankers double up on their steering and navigation controls. In the event of one set breaking down, there is a second set that allows the captain to keep the ship from drifting and causing a collision.

## SAFETY INSPECTIONS

Tankers are inspected regularly to check that machinery is working properly. They are also checked for any signs of rusting or wear and tear that could make a spill more likely.

# OIL TANKERS OF THE FUTURE

In the future, it is possible that fewer oil tankers will be needed. This is because burning oil and other fossil fuels is releasing gases, including carbon dioxide, that store the sun's heat in the atmosphere. This is causing **global warming**, which is making many places warmer and also changing weather patterns worldwide.

## Continued Need for Oil

For now, there are few practical alternatives to standard fuels for vehicles, even though there are various vehicles that run on solar power. So, over the coming decades, we will still rely on oil products. Future tankers could run on liquefied natural gas rather than fuel oil, since burning the gas has lower impact on the environment.

### AFTERLIFE

Rather than scrapping old oil tankers, these massive structures could be used as buildings. People are now imagining the decks as terraces and the cleaned-up insides as housing or shopping malls.

While people still rely on fuels to power their machines, they will need oil tankers to transport oil and its products across oceans.

## Wind Power

Tankers burn a lot of fuel on an ocean journey, contributing to global warming. In the future, these tankers will be able to cruise at top speeds, using less engine power with the help of wind. One option is to use kites. Kites flying hundreds of feet in the air can pick up stronger winds than at the ocean surface. This power can help pull a ship along and reduce fuel costs by more than 10%. For an oil tanker, that could mean saving thousands of dollars day! Another option is to use EnergySails. These are rigid sails mounted on the deck of the oil tanker. The surface also contains **solar cells**, which are devices that can convert the energy in sunlight into electricity. The ship can generate electricity, so it saves on fuel costs.

# GLOSSARY

**alloy** A mix of metals.

**ballast** A weight, such as water, added to a boat to make it more stable.

**beams** Long, strong pieces that give strength to the inside of a structure.

**bow** The front of the boat's hull.

**bow thrusters** Engines in the bow to push the front of a boat to the side.

**bridge** The part of a ship from where the captain and crew operate and maneuver the ship.

**capsizing** Overturning in the water.

**contaminated** Made impure by adding something else.

**corrosion** Destruction of material surfaces by the action of chemicals.

**crude oil** Thick oil taken from the ground.

**deck** The top, main surface of a boat or ship.

**density** A measurement of the amount of material packed into a given volume.

**displaces** Pushes aside.

**drag** The force of friction between a moving object and the substance, such as water, through which it moves.

**forces** Pushes or pulls that can change the way things move.

**fossil fuel** Fuel formed underground naturally from the remains of ancient living things. The process takes millions of years.

**FPSOs** The abbreviation for Floating Production, Storage, and Offloading vessels, which are floating oil depots at sea.

**global warming** The increase in average Earth temperature resulting from use of fuels by people.

**gravity** A downward force pulling any object on Earth's surface or in its atmosphere toward our planet.

**hull** The bottom of a boat.

**liquefied petroleum gas** (LPG) A fuel stored as a liquid but which is burned as a gas.

**pressure** Force.

**propeller** A machine with angled blades that spins to create thrust in water or air.

**pumps** Devices used to suck in liquid.

**refineries** Factories that process crude oil into fuels and other useful products.

**rudders** Devices that are twisted to make boats change direction.

**rust** A red substance formed by the reaction between iron and oxygen. When metal rusts, it gets weaker and can break.

**solar cells** Devices that convert energy in sunlight into electrical energy.

**stern** The back of a boat, which is often blunt, not pointed.

**thrust** A pushing force in one direction.

**upthrust** The force pushing objects up in liquid. It is also known as buoyancy.

**vapor** Gas form of a substance.

**weight** The effect of gravity on the mass of an object.

**winches** Machines, usually electrical, to wind cable or rope in or out.

# FURTHER READING

## Books

Arnold, Quinn M. *Oasis of the Seas* (Now That's Big). Creative Paperbacks, 2017.

Benoit, Peter. *The Exxon Valdez Oil Spill* (True Books: American History). Scholastic, 2011.

Person, Stephen. *Saving Animals from Oil Spills* (Rescuing Animals from Disasters). Bearport Publishing, 2011.

## Websites

Due to the changing nature of Internet links, PowerKids Press has developed an online list of websites related to the subject of this book. This site is updated regularly. Please use this link to access the list: www.powerkidslinks.com/mas/oil

# INDEX